THE
ANTI-RACIST
SOCIAL WORKER
IN PRACTICE

THE ANTI-RACIST SOCIAL WORKER IN PRACTICE

Edited by Nimal Jude, Tanya Moore and Glory Simango

Routledge
Taylor & Francis Group

LONDON AND NEW YORK

Cover design by Out of House Limited

First published 2025
by Routledge
4 Park Square, Milton Park, Abingdon, Oxon OX14 4RN

and by Routledge
605 Third Avenue, New York, NY 10158

Routledge is an imprint of the Taylor & Francis Group, an informa business

© 2025 Shabnam Ahmed, Amos Alake, Lisa Aldridge, Dan Allen, Kristel Campbell-Bobb, Phil Chiza, Clenton Farquharson, Victoria Hart, Allison Hulmes, Nimal Jude, Millie Kerr, Yvonne Mackleworth, Noshin Mohamed, Omar Mohamed, Tanya Moore, Antonia Ogundayisi, Narges Qauyumi, Isaac Samuels, Glory Simango, Jessie Turville, Dr Arlene Weekes and Jo Williams

British Library Cataloguing in Publication Data
A CIP record for this book is available from the British Library

ISBN: 9781916925595 (pbk)
ISBN: 9781041057413 (ebk)

DOI: 10.4324/9781041057413

Text design by Out of House Limited
Typeset in Cabin Condensed Regular
by Newgen Publishing UK

Contents

Dedications

Chapter 1

To my daughter Delilah-Rose for your patience and perseverance, as I strive to make you proud and make your tomorrows much brighter than today.
Millie Kerr

Chapter 2

To Tapi, Giles and the Essex Adult Social Care Senior Practitioner's Network, who have supported and contributed to the thinking in this chapter.
Amos Alake, Phil Chiza, Yvonne Mackleworth, Tanya Moore and Jessie Turville

Chapter 3

For Michelle Simmons-Safo, Rebecca Infanti-Milne and the Hackney Surge Team.
Lisa Aldridge

Chapter 4

To my younger sister, Kazmin, to continue a commitment for an anti-racist world in which she can thrive.
Omar Mohamed

Chapter 5

Dedicated to my daughters, Halo-Reign and My Reign-Beau.
Kristel Campbell-Bobb

Chapter 6

Dedicated to all the formal and informal carers who care for children who have local authority involvement.
Narges Qauyumi

Chapter 7

To my mother, Joana, who passed away in December 2023. She was a woman of compassion and strength, who faced life's challenges with grace and fortitude. Her unwavering support, love and wisdom continue to inspire me every day. This chapter is for her, in honour of her memory and the impact she had on my life.
Clenton Farquharson

Chapter 8

A special thank you to Rebecca Clarkson, Keymn Whervin and Samantha-Jane Ofoegbu for their unwavering support and inspiration on this journey.
Isaac Samuels

Chapter 9

My darling Naomi, may your drom be long and blessed.
Dan Allen and Allison Hulmes

Chapter 10

To my parents, David and Enid Hart. My father, who taught me that being proudly Jewish means standing against all forms of hate and discrimination, and my mother who never had the opportunity to do so.
Victoria Hart

Chapter 11

To our esteemed colleagues, Professor Prospera Tedam, Professor Claudia Bernard and Sharon Jennings, who have all graced us with their wisdom on anti-racist supervision and leadership, making it possible for us to write this chapter.
Shabnam Ahmed and Jo Williams

Chapter 12

To Joy, who always keeps it real and is a real force for change in the social care world!
Antonia Ogundayisi

Chapter 13

To my dear colleague and friend, Geraldine McNally, from our shared personal experiences of discrimination to our unwavering professional mission to champion equity on all fronts, this chapter is dedicated to you as a testament to our journey together.

Working side by side — your insight as Panel Advisor and my role as Independent Chair — we strove to create a better, fairer experience for everyone attending panels. Your dedication, passion and partnership have made this work not only possible but deeply meaningful.
Dr Arlene Weekes

Chapter 14

Dedicated to my son Siyaam — my greatest inspiration and guiding light.
Noshin Mohamed

Chapter 15

For Chris, because of you, things actually changed.
Nimal Jude

All royalties from this book will be going to Social Workers Without Borders.

Social Workers Without Borders is a social work organisation, formed by volunteer social workers across the UK, that uses our professional voices, skills and knowledge to defend and promote fairness and equality for individuals, families and communities impacted by immigration controls. Our vision is for a society where people's self-determination and welfare is not restricted by immigration policy and control. We believe that all individuals, families and communities should have access to social work support from social workers that understand immigration policy and advocate for people's rights and freedoms. There are three strands to our work: campaigning, direct work and education. SWWB campaigns to promote and protect the rights of people with insecure immigration status and to challenge immigration policies that cause hardship, discrimination and injustice. Our 'Direct work' group undertakes and writes expert reports to support people's applications to remain in the UK, or to be reunited with their families. We supervise a network of volunteer social workers to conduct independent social work assessments that are legal-aid funded or free of charge for people who cannot pay for this essential expert evidence. Through our 'Education' group, we share this expert knowledge with the social work sector to support improvements in education and practice.

To become involved please visit www.socialworkerswithoutborders.org.

Meet the storytellers

Shabnam Ahmed MBE
Shabnam is a social worker, doctoral student, and founder of the School of Shabs. Her work focuses on compassionate leadership, anti-racism and supervision. She delivers training nationally on these topics with an aim to support others to create equitable, inclusive and reflective spaces in social work. She has been recognised with an MBE for contributions to social work and serves as an Associate for Research in Practice. As an active member of the Black and Ethnic Minority Professional Symposium (BPS), she led the development of an anti-racist supervision template in collaboration with the group. Her passion lies in advancing equity within professional spaces.

Amos Alake
Amos is a senior social worker with substantial experience in working with children/families and adults with learning disability and autism. He feels blessed to share lived life experiences of work undertaken in a person-centred, anti-discriminatory and empowering way.

Lisa Aldridge
Lisa qualified with an MA in social work in 2000 and has worked within Coram Family and in Children and Families Services across the boroughs of Islington, Camden, Royal Borough of Kensington and Chelsea and London Borough of Hackney. She has been employed as Head of Safeguarding and Quality Assurance in Hackney since 2016. Lisa is currently undertaking her professional doctorate in advanced practice and research in social work and social care at the Tavistock Clinic (2022–26). She uses critical race theory, systemic thinking and critical realism in her thinking and approach, recognising the impact of her Whiteness as a researcher.

Dan Allen
Dan is a social work practitioner and academic with over 20 years of experience focused on improving social work and child protection practices for Romani and Traveller families. He is an established expert in this field, with extensive publications and presentations at prestigious platforms including the European Union Agency for Fundamental Rights, the House of Lords, the Welsh Assembly, and national and international conferences.

Kristel Campbell-Bobb

Kristel is a systemically trained qualified social worker with a BA in psychology and sociology. She holds a CPCAB Accredited Level 2 in counselling skills and has over 20 years of experience in youth criminal justice. She champions critical practice, believing reflection is key to achieving positive outcomes. As a Child Exploitation Consultant Practitioner, Kristel drives best practice and provides reflective supervision for social workers. She is also the Independent Chair for two Youth Justice Management Boards, offering oversight and accountability. A committed advocate for social justice, Kristel works to create positive change for vulnerable young people, promoting fairness and just treatment in all aspects of her practice.

Phil Chiza

After qualifying overseas as an occupational therapist more than 20 years ago, and working in the NHS, private sector and social care, Phil took an opportunity to make a difference by leading on the Race Quest programme in Adult Social Care (ASC) for a local authority. The Quest was introduced as a way of identifying equality, diversity and inclusion issues and opportunities within Adult Social Care. Phil is currently the Development Manager for Race. He is passionate about ensuring that equality issues, especially race, are embedded into his organisation's daily functions and activities. Phil believes racial equity requires a system-wide approach, wider networking, critical reflection and making considered changes. His focus is working effectively across all levels within social care to deliver anti-racist practice and racial equity. He is committed to driving positive change, and promoting equity and inclusion as his long-term ambition.

Clenton Farquharson CBE

Clenton is a visionary leader reimagining health, social care, housing and technology to ensure no one is left behind. As associate director of Think Local Act Personal, he advocates for personalised, inclusive support for disabled people and carers, using AI and digital innovations to empower individuals. His work centres on equity, dignity and co-production, making sure everyone is a partner in shaping their care and support. Driven by a belief in building a better tomorrow, Clenton is guided by the principle of 'I am because we are', emphasising our interconnectedness and the shared responsibility to create a society where all can live glorious ordinary lives with dignity and independence.

Victoria Hart

Victoria is a forensic social worker based in South London, employed within the NHS. She has been practising as a social worker for 25 years and has worked in a variety of adult services and mental health services in the statutory sector (local authority and NHS) as well as in regulation (CQC and Social Work England). She is a founder member of the NHS Jewish Network and the UK Jewish Social Workers Group, of which she has been vice-chair. She has practised as an AMHP (Approved Mental Health Professional), BIA (Best Interests Assessor) and Practice Educator.

Allison Hulmes

Allison is a Welsh Romani social worker and academic; she is co-founder of the Romani and Traveller Social Work Association. Allison's primary focus is radical transformation in social work practice with Romani and Traveller citizens, working to address anti-Romani and anti-Traveller racism in all its manifestations, so that Romani and Traveller people can flourish in their diverse ethnic and cultural identities. Allison is active in preserving her Welsh Kale language and heritage for future generations as a fundamental human right to access one's indigenous languages and stories, as a means of continuing ethnic identity, culture and history.

Nimal Jude

Nimal has 25 years' experience as a registered social worker specialising in multi-agency children's social care, including youth justice, domestic abuse and substance misuse and is also an expert by experience in these areas. She has led pioneering national initiatives and strategic developments, ensuring co-production and inclusion at every step. Nimal supports organisations in evaluating innovative practices. She has developed numerous standards, guidance, post-qualifying frameworks and training packages, and is a qualified workplace coach and action-learning facilitator. Nimal is a member of the Anti-Racist Movement and has given a TEDx talk on organisational culture change.

Millie Kerr

Millie has been working as a qualified social worker for over 30 years, traversing roles from social worker into management and senior leadership positions within local authority children's services, adult services and the charity sector. Millie's career has encompassed child protection, HIV, child asylum, child trafficking, care leavers and Female Genital Mutilation (FGM). She also has expertise in engaging multi-agency partners in change management and intersectionality. Millie is currently a Strategic Anti-Racist lead for a local authority, responsible for developing anti-racist strategies, action plans and training, to aid service improvement across children's services. A key area of her ongoing career objectives is to continue to enhance social justice, anti-racist practice and racial equity nationally, to bring about better support, practice and inclusion for Black and Global Majority children, social workers and communities. Millie is also a member of the British Association of Social Workers (BASW) strategic children and families thematic group and an associate of the East of England LGA cultural awareness hub.

Yvonne Mackleworth

Yvonne qualified in 2004 as a social worker, working through various specialisms and finishing up in the Quality Assurance Team. She enjoys passing on knowledge to help others to gain confidence and self-autonomy. Yvonne has a wide range of interests, from Continuing Health Care to Cultural Awareness. Yvonne promotes and appreciates culture and cultural identity to enable us to understand others and sees this as crucially important within health and social care. She feels that while we do not need to be experts, we do need to be open, respectful and willing to learn.

Noshin Mohamed

Noshin is a dynamic service manager in Quality Assurance for Children and Young People's Services, born and raised in London. A qualified social worker, she gets an adrenaline rush from completing audits and seeing how recommendations lead to improvements for children and families. With a passion for making a difference, one audit at a time, Noshin balances her career with being a mother and stepmother to three wonderful children – and as a reluctant cat owner, she's learned to embrace the chaos. Her love for change-making is matched only by her sense of humour.

Omar Mohamed

Omar is a 24 year-old Asian British male, born and raised in London, with family and ancestral roots from East Africa and India. Omar is a lived experience activist and sibling kinship carer and uses his role as a social worker as a platform to help make changes in the world that link to promoting social justice, equity and human rights. Omar sits on a variety of committees and leadership groups, provides training and consultancy, and regularly contributes to the next generation of social workers through international work and education. Omar regularly publishes contributions to knowledge related to anti-racism and decolonisation, with a drive to continually promote diasporic, embodied and indigenous knowledge.

Tanya Moore

Tanya is a social worker, teacher and academic. She is currently principal social worker for Essex Adult Social Care and doctoral supervisor for The Tavistock and Portman. Tanya is interested in the role of individual social workers as activists for social justice and in the promotion of reflective, theoretically informed practice across social work and social care. She has previously edited the book *Principles of Practice* and co-edited *The Anti-Racist Social Worker* with Glory Simango.

Antonia Ogundayisi

Antonia is an advocate for truth. She is a passionate social care leader and activist with a specialism in youth justice and anti-racist practice. She is committed to empowering Black communities, and supporting children, families and people to reach their full potential and have the right conditions in which to thrive. Antonia is particularly interested in exposing and addressing anti-Blackness and centring the voices of African and Caribbean social workers who are silenced within racial hierarchies. She is currently working for a county council where she has developed and is currently embedding an anti-racist practice strategy within Children and Families Social Care to address the overrepresentation of Black and mixed heritage children in care.

Narges Qauyumi

Narges Qauyumi, born in Kabul, the capital city of Afghanistan, sought asylum in the UK with her family in 2001, entering through the typical routes portrayed in mainstream media. Narges entered residential care at the age of 16. Despite three failed attempts at A levels before embracing social work as a career path, she went on to complete a BA Honours in psychosocial studies at the University of East London, before completing a master's in social work at Nottingham Trent University. Narges qualified as a social worker in 2021 during the Covid-19 pandemic. During her first year of university, Narges became a kinship carer to her sister at the age of 21. After fostering her sister for seven years Narges entered mainstream fostering where she embraced the role of a care experienced foster carer to mainstream teenagers with a local authority for four years. Narges gave up her fostering career to become a Special Guardian to her nephew, caring for a family member for the second time in her life. Narges is part of the Association of Care Experienced Social Care Workers and has made chapter contributions towards *Hidden Narratives of Care Experienced Social Workers*. She is featured in podcasts where she provides her unique insight into the care industry from a position of having been in care, having cared for those most vulnerable and being a professional in a position of power.

Isaac Samuels

Isaac is a disability and social justice activist with a rich background in advocating for social change. Drawing from personal experience of relying on care support and overcoming multiple disadvantages, Isaac champions co-production and ensuring marginalised voices are heard and valued. With a deep belief in storytelling as a catalyst for change, Isaac has dedicated their life to helping others achieve better outcomes, through both their professional work and personal relationships. Passionate about empowering communities, Isaac works tirelessly to dismantle systemic barriers, promote inclusion and uplift individuals, making tangible impacts in social justice spaces and beyond.

Glory Simango

Glory is a social worker and gained her master's in social work at Middlesex University. She is currently practising as a social worker in adult social care. Glory has been working in the social care industry for the past ten years. Glory has a passion for bringing change into people's lives and social justice.

Jessie Turville

Jessie is a practice lead occupational therapist currently working for the Quality Assurance Team for Essex Adult Social Care. Jessie has previous work experience in numerous health settings and special education. Jessie is passionate about inspiring good quality practice for all.

Dr Arlene Weekes

With more than 30 years of experience, Arlene has held a variety of positions in the social work field. She currently distributes her time between chairing fostering panels, facilitating training and lecturing. Arlene engages students by bringing social work practice to life through a student-centred, constructivist and action-learning pedagogy. Arlene's PhD explored how a person's values, attitudes and biography affect their role and decision making. The research concluded that people need to be more self-aware and manage both conscious and unconscious influences; introducing the framework of Effective Personal and Professional Judgement (EPPJ). This framework assists individuals to improve their decisions and actions when meeting the needs of others, through understanding the effect of internal and external influences; *'Increased personal awareness increases professional effectiveness'*.

Jo Williams

Jo is an independent social work consultant, supervisor, coach, educator and author. She has worked in social care and social work settings for 30 years, with a specialist interest in planning adoption and permanence for children and young people in care and reflective, relationship-based supervision and leadership. Jo has always held an interest in diversity, equity and inclusion. As an aunty of three Brown children, she has a particular interest in anti-racism and White allyship. This has influenced her growing interest in anti-racist allyship in social work practice and achieving anti-racist supervision and leadership in organisations.

Foreword

Anti-racism is not an isolated project

I frequently find myself in spaces where the stories of racial trauma penetrate my soul. Whether from students, social workers, managers or senior leaders, the stories of being overlooked, undermined, invisible or hyper-visible are omnipresent. But these are not just stories; they are the 'living' experiences of individuals, families and communities whose dignity, rights and humanity are systematically eroded every day by racism and acts of violence.

I know many people will see the title of this book and hesitate. Some will assume they already 'get it' – that they understand what racism is and have done their part. Others may think anti-racism is not their issue, that it's irrelevant to their lives and work. But the work to become anti-racist is a lifelong endeavour. It's highly complex and deeply connected to everything we do as social workers and allied professionals.

To the Leaders in our sector, the stories in this book are important for you. You might think racism doesn't happen in your organisation. But it does. I guarantee it. This book will help you open up the conversation, find solutions and improve practice.

Anti-racism can't be an isolated project. It requires intentionality, sustained engagement, critical reflection and a willingness to disrupt racist systems and structures. It also requires *recognition, admission and self-critique*. Racism is woven into the fabric of our profession and society. We can't be lukewarm because if we're not actively working against racism, we're allowing it to persist. This is why I'm passionate about the need to keep anti-racism at the heart of our practice, and why this second volume of *The Anti-Racist Social Worker – The Anti-Racist Social Worker in Practice* – is a must-read for all. Its stories and reflections offer real-world examples of how anti-racist practice can and must be done.

The Anti-Racist Movement

It is the stories of pain, struggle, injustice, and of a profound sense of unbelonging that propelled the Anti-Racist Movement (ARM) into formation. The movement is a collective dedicated to creating healing and nurturing spaces for Black women in social work and applied professions. Our mission is to be fearless, joyful and unapologetic while forming a collective resistance. We nurture each other and care deeply, while providing emotional support, professional development and community-building opportunities. We create environments where those affected can come together to reimagine solutions, offer collective care, and – perhaps most powerfully – leave feeling uplifted, joyful and with a renewed sense of hope. I'm proud to see that several members of the ARM collective have contributed chapters to this book.

Who should read this book?

This book is for everyone, regardless of background, experience or beliefs. Whether you've picked this up out of curiosity, duty or necessity, I encourage you to reflect on its lessons and take steps to integrate anti-racist practice into your daily work.

The work of anti-racism is never done. But by reading this book, you're taking one more step on the journey towards creating a more just and equitable world. We owe it to ourselves, to our profession and to the people we serve to keep pushing forward. Together, we are stronger.

Shantel Thomas, Head of Discipline for Social Work
Tavistock and Portman NHS Foundation Trust

About Shantel Thomas

Shantel is a Black woman: UK-born, South London raised, Jamaican parents of African descent. She is a mother, daughter, sister, friend, social work leader, activist and academic. Shantel was previously the UK anti-racism lead for the British Association of Social Workers (BASW) and is now Head of Discipline for Social Work at the Tavistock and Portman NHS Foundation Trust. Shantel is also founder and lead of the Anti-Racist Movement (ARM), a platform dedicated to creating a sacred nurturing and healing space for Black women.

INTRODUCTION

Nimal Jude, Tanya Moore and Glory Simango

In volume one of *The Anti-Racist Social Worker*, we presented stories of anti-racist activism by social workers against the backdrop of the murder of George Floyd and the Covid-19 pandemic. We highlighted the precious energy that drives change and shared stories to encourage individual, organisational and national level anti-racist activism. We asserted that 'anti-racism is a verb not a noun' and left our readers with a call to rise up against racism.

Since its publication, we've been thrilled with the response the book has received and heartened to know it's been used to encourage and inspire social workers, students, educators and service leaders to consider their own part in the creation of an anti-racist society. We've witnessed a variety of anti-racist activity take place, including the creation of policies, listening groups, forums and actions plans. We've been excited to see where this is leading to actual progress.

The urgency to challenge racism in our practice, education and research has become more widely understood, but as practitioners we still need a clear indication of what social workers can actually *do* to challenge explicit and implicit racism in practice. Are we fully aware of how racism can manifest in our direct work with people and do we have the confidence and skills to challenge the discrimination, inequality and injustice that we know is ingrained in our systems? Despite the optimism and increased activity in 2021, racism has not been eradicated and, in some areas, has even worsened. It's disheartening to see that progress has been slow, but acknowledging these issues is a crucial step towards meaningful change.

The Anti-Racist Social Worker in Practice is our response to this need. It's a suggested 'how-to' for anti-racist practice. As a collection of practice stories and experiences written by social work practitioners and academics as well as by people who draw on social care services, each chapter takes an element of practice, considers it through an anti-racist lens and demonstrates the practical steps we can take to challenge racist assumptions, structures and approaches. We offer these to equip practitioners with the means to make practical sense of the growing consensus on the need for anti-racist practice in social work. We hope this book supports readers to reflect on their own practice and organisational systems and shows how anti-racism can be woven into daily practice.

Each chapter tells a story that demonstrates anti-racist practice and high-lights specific in-roads to anti-racist practice for the reader. Some of the stories are of the authors' own experiences. But where written about others, the stories are an amalgamation of different people and names and identifying features have been changed. We hope these stories provide heart, care and hope and, importantly, a counter-narrative to any assumption that racist systems and structures can't be challenged by practice. Each chapter concludes with critically reflective questions to help to develop thinking about how we can each build anti-racism into our own practice. We invite our readers to share these stories and ideas with colleagues, students, managers and leaders while continuing to develop the thinking offered here by opening up conversations and debates that lead to practice development and action.

We'd like to thank each of our storytellers for their courage in offering a path for anti-racist practice. And we'd like to thank each of our readers for their determination to be an active part of the movement for anti-racist change.

Nimal, Tanya and Glory

CHAPTER 1

ASSESSING THE NEEDS OF BLACK AND GLOBAL MAJORITY CHILDREN THROUGH AN ANTI-RACIST LENS

Millie Kerr

...little children will one day live in a nation where they will not be judged by the color of their skin, but by the content of their character.

– Dr Martin Luther King, 1963

Introduction

As social workers, we need to continually develop our lens of curiosity. Our thinking should diversify away from White Eurocentric social work models and recognise the othering faced by people from Black and Global Majority backgrounds and religions. This is anti-racist practice, and just as safeguarding children is everyone's business, so is working in an anti-racist way.

As the Strategic Anti-Racist lead for Brighton and Hove City Council, my role is to lead change towards improved outcomes for Black and Global Majority children and families. As part of the senior leadership team I develop anti-racist strategies and action plans to develop the workforce to benefit children and young people.

CASE STORY

Identity and intersectionality: I am more than just the colour of my skin

We've taken an intersectional approach to looking at race, culture and the identity of the children, young people and families we serve. As part of a Whole System Review for a father who had experienced stereotyping and racism, I worked with the network on building trust and cultural understanding within our social work and child proceedings processes.

This father had the intersectional identities of being Black, African, a man and a Christian. English was his second language and he came from a middle-class background but was deemed working class in the UK. He had a Work Visa and was subject to immigration control. The father had separated from his British partner and was seeking custody of his child, who was now in foster care as her mother was unable to care for her. The father's experience of social care and the family court process had been difficult. Assumptions were made that because of his African culture, he would hit his daughter, and he was regarded as 'loud'. His immigration status was considered a concern and he hadn't been given access to interpreters or effective communication with his lawyers.

In this case, however, there was a positive result and the father did gain custody of his daughter. Later, he agreed I could interview him so we could learn from his experiences of our systems. The interview highlighted the need for (i) consideration of the intersecting experiences of race, class and gender for Black dads, (ii) curiosity about differences relating to culture, parenting styles, language and stereotypes and (iii) better communication and more time to support families experiencing discrimination and racism from the systems set up to support them.

There was consensus that this father deserved better, that we needed an anti-racist approach to family court proceedings, and a decision was made to develop an Anti-Racist Practice Statement for the family courts. I was instrumental in developing this in partnership with other social work managers, lawyers, barristers and judges. The aim was to create better understanding for professionals and a more equitable experience for Black and Global Majority children and families going through family proceedings. The Anti-Racist Practice Statement for the Family Court (Family Justice Quality Circle, 2022) was later ratified for use in the Sussex Family Courts, as well as within children's social care.

Part of the development work was to look at anti-racist practice more holistically and to consider differing cultural identity needs and parenting styles as well as how social workers could support White parents and foster carers in enhancing children's cultural identity. We also wanted to challenge racism within our systems beyond just looking at linguistic and religious needs. We emphasised the importance of confidence and self-worth and highlighted the need for Black and mixed heritage children to have their hair care needs properly met. We now hold Black hair care workshops for White and Black foster carers of Black and mixed heritage children.

Anti-racist social work starts with looking at the self

Embedding anti-racist practice throughout our services has to start with the self and with recognition of the biases, prejudices, assumptions and stereotypical labels we may ascribe to Black and Global Majority children and families. These labels can be born out of White supremacist ideology and the negative perspectives fed to us through the media. The development of an anti-racist project board to drive forward our action plan has been key to enhancing anti-racist practice within the workforce here in Brighton and Hove. The *Me and my White Supremacy* workbook (Saad, 2020) has been rolled out to the whole workforce, from senior leaders to our business support staff. We also hold regular anti-racist discussion groups, looking at specific topics to enhance practice, such as adultification bias, working with Black dads, transracial/bi-racial adoptions and the overrepresentation of Black and mixed heritage children in school exclusions.

Discussing White privilege, supremacy and fragility is not an attack on Whiteness. It's an opportunity to look at how White privilege in systems and wider society can view people from different cultural and ethnic groups through a stereotypical or inferiority lens. Teaching about this in universities would help social work students understand where biases and racist ideology come from and would help them unlearn some of the negative perspectives held. Leaning into the discomfort of talking about self, race and racism can only enhance overall social work practice going forward.

If strategic action is to be monitored and progressed, it's essential to have senior leadership commitment to progressing anti-racist practice. Brighton and Hove council has made a public commitment to becoming an anti-racist local authority and this provides a good starting point for change, although we know it's going to be a long journey.

Are you assessing Black children and families through a deficit lens?

Assessments of Black and Global Majority children must consider identity, culture, religion, racial trauma, adultification and intersectional identity. We must add the richness and vibrancy of traditions and cultures outside of Eurocentric values to our assessment repertoire, so more positive approaches to direct work can be developed. We have an abundance of evidence on the overrepresentation of Black children in school exclusions, youth justice and the care system. We must reflect on racialised children and their family's needs in terms of their strengths, aspirations and achievements. Curiosity about what we see and hear is fundamental so as not to see Blackness or ethnicity through stereotypical concepts, as a problem or through a 'deficit' or 'inferior' lens.

In Brighton and Hove, we're building our understanding of the adultification bias around Black and Global Majority children and we're focusing on social workers' development of anti-racist practice. Social workers start from the premise that Black and Global Majority children and families have lived experience of racism and may be impacted by racial trauma. We consider this in our assessments and interactions and we seek to understand the causes of issues and to not respond to and judge behaviours in isolation.

We recently organised an engagement event, to hear Black and Global Majority young people's views on the services they receive. Although there was a sense there had been some improvements, the event confirmed the need for ongoing work to tackle experiences of racism in many of our institutions. This includes the need for professionals to examine the cause of young people's behaviour and the need for preventative measures including mental health support, that understand the impact of racial trauma. It requires individual and organisational understanding of the cumulative impact of unaddressed stereotyping and racism that may be born out of repeated school exclusions, stop and search, racist bullying, the experience of being an asylum seeker, islamophobia and being criminalised in the youth justice system.

Anti-racist recording

It's important for us to review the language we use in our written work and assessments to avoid unwittingly stereotyping, labelling, judging or discriminating against the very young people we're trying to support. To aid reflection and change, I often provide social workers with examples of discriminatory or adultifying language that's been used in referrals or reports.

An example might be:

The young person of African Caribbean heritage was being argumentative, loud and aggressive.

Why was the young person being 'loud and aggressive'? What do we mean by 'argumentative'? What was the cause, looking through a trauma/racial trauma lens? What's meant by 'loud' and what context can be given for 'aggressive'? Could 'aggressive' be reworded to 'frustrated'? Did the young person feel listened to?

Another might be:

Dad presented as a big Black angry man, at the news of his child coming into care.

Why do we not also describe White dads as 'a big White angry man'? Is there fear or a lack of confidence around working with Black dads/men and dads in general? Could the presentation be frustration about not feeling listened to or included in assessments in comparison to mothers?

The way we use language is important, and we must give our assessments more attention when describing people and their behaviours, in a trauma-informed way.

We must 'Listen', be 'Curious' and take 'Time' to hear the stories, experiences and cultural perspectives of Black and Global Majority children and families. This is particularly pertinent when working with people whose first language is not English and where customs may differ from our own. We might sit with the discomfort of views that we are or the organisation we work for is racist. We can learn from such instances and ask young people and families what they'd like us to do differently. This will aid service improvements and change and remind us that we're working towards social justice for all!

Anti-racist practice is everyone's business

We've used learning from serious case reviews such as Child Q (Gamble and McCallum, 2022) and Child Delta (Carmi, 2022) to develop our understanding of Black children's lived experiences and to improve our practice and service provision. We can't do this alone and need allies working with us to impact change and improve the lives of young people. Work with partner agencies and community groups is essential so part of my role is to develop strategies and deliver anti-racist workshops across services.

We'll continue to arrange engagement events to listen and learn from the challenges and feelings of young people and the wider community and we'll include them in co-production opportunities to build and rebuild trust within our Global Majority communities.

We must create safe spaces for anti-racist practice to flourish

For Black and Global Majority children to thrive and not just survive in a world that sometimes feels stacked against them, we must engage in the discomfort of uncomfortable conversations about race and racism. This is imperative if we're going to progress inclusivity and equity and if we're to bring about a sense of belonging for Black and Global Majority children and young people.

Moving from '*I'm not racist*' to '*becoming anti-racist*' in our practice means looking inwards at our biases and beliefs to grow confidence in challenging racism and injustice. Creating safe, reflective spaces to support difficult conversations about race and racism has been key to developing and progressing anti-racist practice within children's services in Brighton & Hove City Council. We've a long way to go, and we're not complacent. We're currently embedding anti-racist practice in social work case discussions, team meetings, supervision, reflective discussions, Personal Development Plans and in regular workshops. We're also providing the support needed for our Black and Global Majority staff and international social workers, to enable them to thrive, develop and progress within the local authority.

Sustaining anti-racist social work to improve outcomes for our children requires us to turn our strategies into action, work in partnership and demonstrate a willingness to learn from our mistakes. What action are you going to take to enhance anti-racist practice within your organisation?

Reflective questions to move us forward

1. What does your **culture and identity** mean to you? How would you write about this if you were discussing yourself?

2. How would you explore and write about a young Black person's identity within your assessments, through an **intersectional lens**?

3. Do you feel **confident** in assessing the needs of Black and Global Majority children and young people? If yes, what makes you confident? If you don't feel confident, what additional learning and support do you need for yourself and from your **organisation** to enhance your practice?

Addendum

In the aftermath of summer 2024, when we witnessed far right violence, islamophobia, anti-immigration and racism impact our communities, we must reflect on the effect this has had. Racist ideology and othering is at epidemic proportions. We need to do everything we can, as professionals, to halt intergenerational dislike and racist hate of others. How will we support our children and families to be anti-racist? What action will you take to challenge the racist views of the young people and parents you may be working with? Black, Global Majority, and Muslim communities don't have the White privilege, of not having to tell your children they can't go out to play for fear of them being harmed because of the colour of their skin or because you wear a hijab. Social workers, multi-agency partners and education providers must work to educate our children and families about compassion, empathy and inclusion.

We can all do better as allies and partners working in solidarity against hate and racism.

> If you are disgusted by what you see, and if you feel the fire coursing through your veins, then it's up to you. You don't have to be the leader of a global movement or a household name. It can be as small scale as chipping away at the warped power relations in your workplace. It can be passing on knowledge and skills to those who wouldn't access them otherwise. It can be creative. It can be informal. It can be your job. It doesn't matter what it is, as long as you're doing something.
>
> – Reni Eddo-Lodge

Further reading

Bernard, C and Harris, P (2016) *Safeguarding Black Children, Good Practice in Child Protection*. London: Jessica Kingsley Publishers.

Bonsu, N and Smith, E (2023) Understanding, Exploring and Supporting Children's Identity Development: Practice Tool. Research in Practice. Available at: www.researchinpractice.org.uk/children/publications/2023/september/understanding-exploring-and-supporting-children-s-identity-development-practice-tool-2023/ (accessed 7 January 2025).

Coram, BAAF (2021) Progressing Anti-racist Practice in the Family Justice System. Available at: https://corambaaf.org.uk/progressing-anti-racist-practice-family-justice-system (accessed 7 January 2025).

Davis, J (2022) Adultification Bias within Child Protection and Safeguarding. HM Inspectorate of Probation. Available at: www.justiceinspectorates.gov.uk/hmiprobation/wp-content/uploads/sites/5/2022/06/Academic-Insights-Adultification-bias-within-child-protection-and-safeguarding.pdf (accessed 7 January 2025).

IICSA (2021) Engagement with Support Services for Ethnic Minority Communities. Available at: https://webarchive.nationalarchives.gov.uk/ukgwa/20221216171902/https://www.iicsa.org.uk/key-documents/26008/view/engagement-report-ethnic-minority-communities-29-april-2021.pdf (accessed 7 January 2025).

Sweeney, S and Matthews, Z (2017) A Guide for Professionals Working with Gypsies, Roma and Travellers in Children's Services. Friends, Families and Travellers. www.gypsy-traveller.org/resource/a-guide-for-professionals-working-with-gypsies-roma-and-travellers-in-children%C2%92s-services/ (accessed 7 January 2025).

Wroe, L, Larkin, R and Maglajlic, R A (2019) *Social Work with Refugees, Asylum Seekers and Migrants*. London: Jessica Kingsley Publishers. https://afroribooks.co.uk/.

References

Carmi, E (2022) *Local Child Safeguarding Practice Review Child Delta*. Brighton & Hove Safeguarding Children Partnership. www.bhscp.org.uk/wp-content/uploads/sites/3/2022/11/Lead-Partner-FINAL-REPORT-02.11.22-v4.pdf (accessed 7 January 2025).

Eddo-Lodge, R (2018) *Why I'm No Longer Talking to White People About Race*. London: Bloomsbury Publishing, pp 223–4.

Family Justice Quality Circle (2022) Family Court Anti-Racist Practice Statement. www.sussexfamilyjusticeboard.org.uk/wp-content/uploads/2023/08/Family-Court-anti-racist-practice-statement-Final-app-FJYPB-00.12.2022.docx (accessed 7 January 2025).

Gamble, J and McCallum, R (2022) Local Child Safeguarding Practice Review: Child Q. City and Hackney Safeguarding Children Partnership. https://chscp.org.uk/wp-content/uploads/2022/03/Child-Q-PUBLISHED-14-March-22.pdf (accessed 7 January 2025).

Saad, L (2020) *Me and My White Supremacy*. London: Quercus Editions Ltd.

CHAPTER 2

CONVERSATIONS ABOUT CULTURE IN ADULT SOCIAL CARE

Amos Alake, Phil Chiza, Yvonne Mackleworth,
Tanya Moore and Jessie Turville

The authors of this chapter are three social workers (Amos, Tanya and Yvonne) and two occupational therapists (Jessie and Phil). All of us have roles in supporting and developing social care practice. Amos is a senior social worker, Jessie and Yvonne are practice leads in our Quality Assurance Team, Phil is the anti-racist manager and Tanya is the principal social worker. We all work in Essex Adult Social Care.

We believe that culture is central to the core of who we are and that good person-centred practice is built on an understanding of what's important to the person drawing on support. But we understand that if as practitioners, we don't know how to ask questions about culture, we can inadvertently make assumptions about what's important and this can lead to us imposing expectations and norms of our own culture onto another. We consider this to be oppressive practice and where the person about whom we're making assumptions is from an ethnically marginalised background, we consider this imposition to be racist.

The following story was told by Amos at a meeting of our adult social care senior practitioners forum.

CASE STORY

I visited a lady who had been staying in a temporary home for a few months. I'd been asked to do a review because things were finally getting moving and there was a chance of a permanent home for her on the horizon.

I asked her what kind of help she might need in the future to help her settle into her own home. We talked about this for a while, but while the lady was recorded as being 'White British', I'd noticed she had darker skin and wondered whether she was of southern European origin. I asked her how she would describe her ethnicity. She said her mother was Welsh and her dad was from Dominica. She told me she relates to both parts of her identity. The lady told me she was a bit unhappy and a bit depressed with where she was currently living. She said this was because the food wasn't very good; she likes Caribbean food and there was none available. She also said she didn't have access to the right creams to protect her skin and her hair wasn't being properly looked after. The lady told me there was no one working in the home who knew how to look after Black skin and hair.

The support worker was surprised. They'd never queried the record of 'White British'. They didn't realise she had either Dominican or Welsh heritage and they'd never considered the appropriateness of the food on offer in the house. Following an animated discussion with the lady and her support worker, it was decided they might order in some Caribbean food either from a takeaway or from a Caribbean supermarket. They also started planning an evening out at a Caribbean restaurant. They also made enquiries about booking an appointment with a Caribbean hairdresser so the lady could be seen by a specialist stylist who knew what they were doing.

I could see the lady was beginning to cry and I asked her what was wrong. She said nobody had ever asked her about her ethnicity before. This lady presents such that she could be seen as White, but I'd noticed her skin

> *pigmentation. This had raised my curiosity and so I'd asked the question. I hadn't realised that a part of her heritage was Dominican. But it was very important to her to be able to talk about it.*
>
> *We shouldn't be afraid to ask a question when it comes to race and ethnicity. It's easy to assume and this can lead to discriminatory practice that denies people important aspects of their identity.*

It's painful to imagine how this lady might have felt to have such an important element of herself overlooked. It impacted the way she was seen, the assumptions about who she was and also the physical care she received in terms of the food she was offered and the way her skin and hair were cared for. It made us consider how easy it is, if we're part of the dominant culture, to see only ourselves in others. This lady was recorded as White British, and in all the years she'd been supported by Adult Social Care nobody had recognised any difference. She'd been expected to conform to the expected White norm, but how can we work with a person, especially when we're supporting them with life decisions, without understanding what's important to them, without knowing about and working to meet their cultural needs?

For this lady, it took Amos, who's a Black social worker, to notice her difference, to be curious and to have the confidence to ask her for her story. And it was this lady's story that helped us understand how our curiosity about cultural needs is an essential element of anti-racist practice.

Practitioners all want to be better at asking about people's cultural needs but there's some anxiety and apprehension, particularly among White social workers, about getting this wrong and causing offence. But if we let our discomfort and fear of getting it wrong stop us having conversations about culture, we're failing in our duty to ensure cultural needs are being addressed and also failing in our imperative to challenge racism. Not meeting person-centred cultural needs is oppressive practice, as it means we often inadvertently end up imposing our own culture onto others and this becomes racist practice.

Perhaps it's no surprise that it took a Black social worker to notice the lady wasn't White. When we fail to see colour, our racial 'colour blindness' may be a result of our ability to see character rather than the colour of skin, but on a deeper level, it might be discomfort in difference and, for White social workers, even a denial of the disadvantage that can be caused by race.

Discomfort or failure in social workers to either see or ask about race and culture means failure to recognise the trauma and inequality associated with ethnic marginalisation. It can be seen as an assertion of White privilege for White social workers to opt out of conversations or considerations about race, culture and difference as this option can never be made available to anyone marginalised by the colour of their skin.

But there's a deeper and more insidious danger in any failure to recognise difference. When we fail to acknowledge ethnic marginalisation, we might also fail to recognise any structural disadvantage it brings and may mistakenly individualise the problems. So, we may 'blame' the individual for issues that have a much wider structural cause. In other words, we might, for example, think at some level that the poverty experienced by a particular family is the result of a lifestyle choice or lack of work ethic/ambition and miss the connection to the wider disparity in educational, employment and housing opportunities for some ethnically marginalised groups.

So, we think conversations about culture are essential to anti-racist practice.

Conversations about culture

People and their care givers won't always be from the same cultural background, and there will be differences even between people with shared culture. The only way we can understand a person's culture is to hear it from them, their loved ones or others who have cultural needs in common.

To help build our confidence as practitioners recognising difference and initiating conversations, we've found it helpful to look inwards and reflect on our own cultural needs. Particularly for those of us who are White as this helps us unpick the unspoken (and oppressive) assumption that our way of being is 'the normal way'. Failure to do this can translate into oppressive practice in which people are expected to fit into cultural structures designed for the dominant group. This would be particularly damaging and frightening when we're at our most vulnerable, such as when needing to draw upon social care.

With other practitioners in Essex Adult Social Care, we've considered what we might need our care givers to know should we move into a residential or nursing home. Our answers gave vibrant insight into each other's lives as colleagues across our network talked about the languages we speak at home, the people we live with, the food we eat, the music we listen to, the things we enjoy as well as the behaviours of others we can't tolerate. We learned about each other's celebrations, rituals, observances, habits, humour and the calendars by which we each organise our lives. All of these elements and more express our differences and reveal the culture that feels 'normal' to each of us. But how do we translate this recognition of our own culture into an anti-oppressive and anti-racist appreciation of the culture of others?

For Amos and the lady in our case story, the answer lay in sound person-centred practice. Amos' interest in the lady was friendly, respectful and genuine. He made no assumptions. He asked open questions and listened carefully to her answers, noticing the hints she gave about how she manages to cope. He ensured the lady remained in control of the direction the conversation took. We consider this to be relational and strengths-based practice. But relational practice involves an examination of the relationship co-created between the person and practitioner. And it was in authentic attendance to his respectful curiosity and his awareness of the difference between them that Amos was able to ask the questions that allowed the lady to reveal this essential element of her identity.

So often, the 'invisible culture' is the White, Western culture. Its prevalence enables its dominance. To actively see, value and support difference is to offer a person-centred response to the diverse needs of the people who draw on social care. But it's also to disrupt the unspoken assumption of conformity to the dominant culture and to respond to the very different and unequal contexts within which we operate. We consider this to be a basic element of anti-racist practice in adult social care.

Reflective questions to move us forward

1. What are your cultural needs?

2. How comfortable do you feel in having conversations about culture?

3. What assumptions do you think your service might make about the cultural needs of others?

CHAPTER 3

THE INTERSECTION OF RACISM AND POVERTY: WHAT DIFFERENCE CAN WE MAKE?

Lisa Aldridge

Introduction

It's with great privilege that I'm writing this chapter which considers the role of social work in addressing racism and poverty. I'm fortunate to work in a local authority that has a determined Poverty Reduction strategy and passed a political motion and explicit commitment to anti-racism in 2021. We talk about racism, beyond the notions of equality, diversity and inclusion, acknowledging those concepts in themselves don't explicitly address racism. As a White senior lead, I'm conscious of the privilege that Whiteness gives me. I have no experience of racism and know my White lens is limiting. I know what it's like to experience material childhood poverty, but my experience of class disadvantage pales into insignificance in the context of the deadly impact of systemic racism. I seek to tune into my learned racism to unlearn and redress proactively. I'm writing this chapter to utilise the power that my position gives me, making one small contribution to change.

In this chapter, I look at the intersection of racism and poverty and how our understanding of systemic systems of oppression should inform and shape social work practice. I highlight a best practice example that uses principles of anti-racist and poverty-aware practice to respond to the sharp increase in children's acute mental health presentations.

A note on language: throughout this chapter, I use the term 'Black' as a political statement of a collective of people who experience racism and are racialised as 'other'. I use the term 'Black and Global Majority' as coined by Rosemary Campbell-Stephens (2021) to reverse the minoritisation of the common language used such as 'ethnic minority' and to recentre 85 per cent of the world's population, though where quoting authors, I adhere to their use of language.

The UK context

An astounding 4.3 million children are now growing up in poverty in the UK, which means that 30 per cent of children in an average classroom are living in poverty (Child Poverty Action Group [CPAG], nda). Systemic racism means a disproportionate 47 per cent of children from Black and minority ethnic groups are living in poverty, compared to 24 per cent of White children (CPAG, nda). Racism is a form of harm that has a profound impact on physical and mental health (Priest et al, 2013), educational outcomes (Demie, 2019), employment (Goodfellow and Macfarlane, 2018), and criminal justice outcomes for our children (Phillips and Bowling, 2017), further compounded by experiences of poverty.

The connection between poverty and its disproportionate impact on Black and Global Majority people is no accident. Western capitalism created wealth through the trans-Atlantic slave trade, thriving upon a theory of 'race' that created White supremacy, maintaining class oppression and subjugating Black and Global Majority 'others' (Akala, 2019; Olusoga, 2021). Conservative Government social policy exacerbated poverty through the cruel introduction of the two-child limit for child benefits, the bedroom tax, the housing benefit cap, and migration from legacy benefits to Universal Credit lacking transitional protection. According to We Are Citizens Advice (2023), the changes to tax benefits in the last decade have resulted in:

- Black families being £1,635 less well off;
- Asian families being £728 less well off;
- White families being £454 less well off.

In 2023 an Office for National Statistics survey into the cost of living crisis found that about half of Asian or British Asian adults, and 47 per cent of Black, African, Caribbean, or Black British adults, were struggling to afford their rent or mortgage payments, compared with 33 per cent of White adults. The data speaks for itself. The denial of systemic racism declared through the government-commissioned Sewell report (2021) only served to validate its ignorance of structural discrimination and the role that it plays in social policy.

Social work principles, values and ethics

Many of us, if not all, decide to enter social work to 'make a difference', and our professional standards require us to promote the rights, strengths and well-being of people, families and communities (Social Work England, 2019).

There is, however, a disconnect between our profession's expressed values and, at times, the impact of our practice. Research confirms the existence of racism towards Black and Global Majority people including through overt, and covert, practices in social work (Bernard, 2020). Black children are over-represented within the care system within the UK, creating a sense of powerlessness and shame for Black parents (Barn et al, 2006). Black and Global Majority social work students in the UK experience hostility and are othered, with 'race' and racism being a taboo subject left undiscussed and unaddressed (Obasi, 2022). Against all our best intentions, we (in particular White social workers) are perpetuating harm to our colleagues, our children and our families.

Our profession has been insufficiently anti-racist in its thinking and practice. We have a history of focusing on cultural competence and multiculturalism, but cultural awareness training is limited in promoting anti-racist activism (Jeffrey, 2005). Further to this, the evident relationship between poverty, inequality and child protection evidences that poverty creates increased parental stress, which can increase the risk of harm, but also, perversely, that our individualised and often blaming child protection system creates the risk of denying the impact of poverty and wider social structural harm (Featherstone et al, 2018).

And the connection with poverty-aware practice?

Krumer-Nevo's (2020) Poverty-Aware Social Work Paradigm focuses on the systemic oppression created through poverty and identifies this as a violation of human rights. With echoes of radical pre-Thatcherite social work in the UK, the approach demands that we stand in solidarity and position ourselves alongside families to resist poverty and create change. The approach couples rights-based practice with relational practice. It offers an appreciation of the emotional pain created by poverty and the struggle to survive. It builds upon families' actions to resist poverty – as such, it is a strengths-based approach that acknowledges families' expertise in their own lives.

I've previously written about poverty (Aldridge, 2023, pp 95–102) and high-lighted some of the numerous steps social workers can take to alleviate material poverty. This can include:

- support for Universal Credit migration and council tax rebates;
- supporting families on low incomes to access free school meals for families, including families with no recourse to public funds;
- ensuring access to school uniform grants which are not dependent upon free school meal access;
- 15 hours of free childcare and additional food vouchers for holiday breaks for children aged two and over where families receive benefits or are working and receiving a low-income;
- signposting to local food banks, community kitchens and community food shops that offer cultural food products;
- access to hardship funds for families with no recourse to public funds;
- direct payments for disabled children being used by families flexibly for immediate practical needs alongside care and support needs;
- use of Section 17 financial support for urgent practical items for children such as clothing, bedding, food vouchers or money for gas and electric payment meters;
- charity grant applications to support families in purchasing furniture, white goods or paint for redecorating.

Beyond this, our social work skills and values are founded upon relationships – our stance and approach to working with families are as impactful as the practical resources we can offer. If we're to be anti-racist we also need to be trauma-informed, recognising the stigma, shame and harm caused by poverty as a societal problem, and position ourselves alongside families in solidarity to challenge social injustice. This means getting alongside families to understand their stories and experiences as a priority rather than simply imposing our agendas based upon referrals from partner agencies.

CASE STORY

Best practice from Hackney

The Surge Team was created in Hackney in 2021 in response to the rapid increase in referrals for children with acute mental health needs approaching a need for Tier 4 CAMHS inpatient services. A multidisciplinary team within Children and Families Services included clinical therapists, a mental health nurse, social workers and youth workers providing intensive support with clinical oversight. The majority of children referred were from Black and Global Majority backgrounds, working class, and experiencing both systemic racism and material poverty as mutually reinforcing dynamics.

Systemic racism and Whiteness were core considerations from the outset of creating the Surge Team with a determination to 'cultivate a shared understanding and tolerance of talking about the unspoken, the difficult and the uncomfortable' (Context 192, p 30). Recruitment was intentional, ensuring that staff authentically understood the reality of families' lived experiences of everyday racism. The senior manager leading the service was White and addressed the power dynamics implicit in her skin colour by acknowledging her privilege and racism and by encouraging Black and Global Majority staff to challenge both her and other White members of staff. There was acknowledgement

$\longrightarrow$

that it would take time and meaningful development of relationships to develop trust, with the most senior Black manager understandably feeling sceptical in the context of experiencing a lifetime of racism in the workplace. Careful consideration was given to the creation of psychological safety in the relationships between Black and White colleagues. Space and permission was supported for Black colleagues to be authentic and resist partnership criticisms where they might not conform to the expected White norms of practice (including systems that demand we work fast, give little space for thinking, present ourselves in line with Eurocentric norms, etc). Quickly recognising the impact of vicarious racialised trauma through their practice, a safe reflective space was created for practitioners to share, reflect and heal. Additional time and support was given by managers to Black and Global Majority staff in the team.

These actions made it possible for Black professionals to bring their full selves to work as Black women, and this became a defining feature of the service and its ability to respond effectively to Black families experiencing poverty.

What is the essence of this practice?

This mindset and culture enabled practitioners to engage with the systemic oppression in families' lives, focusing on developing nurturing, trusting, respectful and compassionate relationships from the outset. Practitioners listened to families' narratives, giving them time and space to explain their stories. Conversations were normalised, rather than questioning as part of a set agenda. In line with the Poverty-Aware Paradigm (Krumer-Nevo, 2020), practitioners took a strengths-based approach, centring on self-determination and positive risk-taking to enable families to take charge of their own lives. One parent said, 'Surge has been my safety blanket. The help has been outstanding, I want to know if I can buy some more Surge time. For the first time, I had someone who gave time to me as a parent and was not judgemental.'

Practitioners were clear they didn't have all of the answers – families held most of these. In the context of unresolved trauma, deep poverty practitioners helped to repair family relationships seeking to rebuild the village that is needed to raise a child. Recognising the poverty of one parent who worked long hours and the judgemental statement of another professional that this father 'couldn't be bothered' to engage, charity grants were mobilised to ensure the family's home had essential equipment (a cooker and fridge). Instead of expecting the father to leave work to come to appointments, practitioners met him near his work and this led to the additional engagement of his relative, who worked nearby, to support the family too. Another parent was supported to address their experiences of racism at work. This reduced their distress and anxiety, improved their family relationships and reduced the future risk of feeling the need to leave employment due to racism.

Practitioners acknowledged families' experiences of being let down by services, identified gaps in support, strongly advocated for effective services and engaged in thinking about the stigma attached to traditional mental health and social care services. The team sought to interrupt any service narratives that pathologised parenting, creating new humanistic narratives that recognised parents' strengths and the desire to do their best in the context of the limited resources available to them. This was ethical practice in action.

Relationships were paramount, advocating for families who had often struggled for years. Surge challenged statutory services to radically change their approach to engaging and supporting families experiencing structural poverty and racism. Another parent said, 'Surge has helped me in a way no other service has been able to. It has also helped [child] ... to want better for herself and stop self-harming...'

Surge worked alongside statutory social workers to ensure families could access practical and financial resources and created a budget to buy food and hair care products for children. There was an understanding that 'You can't do therapy with a hungry child', and sharing food and eating together was part of the support, relationship and intervention.

It's clear that Surge's explicitly anti-racist and poverty-informed approach to practice was largely successful and could support families to create change. But all this was only possible because of the anti-racist approach to creating and running the team in which team members could feel their protection, and dignity, were upheld.

Conclusion

The context of austerity, years of right-wing rule and neglect of public services have pushed families and services to the brink of collapse. Despite this context, we can still centre compassionate, anti-racist and poverty-informed practice to stand in solidarity, advocate and create change for our children and families. We can resist the status quo, centre our ethics and values and dismantle systems of Whiteness within our practice. To do so requires our collective commitment and accountability to create change.

Reflective questions to move us forward

1. How do you locate yourself, your ethnicity and your position in conversations with children, families and colleagues?

2. What do you do to create psychological safety as part of ethical practice?

3. What can you do to be poverty-informed and proactively anti-racist to stand in solidarity with children, families and colleagues?

References

Akala (2019) *Natives: Race and Class in the Ruins of Empire*. London: Two Roads.

Aldridge, L (2023) Poverty and the Need for Radical Relational Practice. In Moore, T (ed) *Principles of Practice* (pp 95–102). St Albans: Critical Publishing.

Barn, R, Ladino, C and Rogers, B (2006) *Parenting in Multi-Racial Britain*. London: NCH.

Bernard, C (2020) Practice Supervisors Development Programme – Resources for Managers of Practice Supervisors: Addressing Barriers to the Progression of Black and Minority Ethnic Social Workers to Leadership Roles. *Department for Education.*

Campbell-Stephens, R M (2021) Introduction: Global Majority Decolonising Narratives. *Educational Leadership and the Global Majority: Decolonising Narratives*. Cham: Palgrave MacMillan, pp 1–21.

Child Poverty Action Group (CPAG) (nda) Child Poverty Facts and Figures. [online] Available at: https://cpag.org.uk/child-poverty/poverty-facts-and-figures (accessed 7 January 2025).

Context 192 (April 2024) Reflections from the Surge Team in Hackney. Association for Family Therapy and Systemic Practice. Available at: www.aft.org.uk/page/Context (accessed 3 May 2024).

Demie, F (2019) Raising Achievement of Black Caribbean Pupils: Good Practice for Developing Leadership Capacity and Workforce Diversity in Schools. *School Leadership & Management*, 39(1): 5–25.

Dominelli, L (2017) *Anti-Racist Social Work*. London: Bloomsbury Publishing Plc.

Featherstone, B, Gupta, A, Morris, K and White, S (2018) *Protecting Children: A Social Model*. Bristol: Policy Press.

Goodfellow, M and Macfarlane, L (2018) Race and Racism in the UK. In Macfarlane, L (ed) *New Thinking for the British Economy* (pp 150–9). London: Open Democracy.

Jeffrey, D (2005) 'What Good is Anti-Racist Social Work If You Can't Master It?' Exploring a Paradox in Social Work Education. *Race Ethnicity and Education*, 8(4): 409–25.

Krumer-Nevo, M (2016) Poverty-Aware Social Work: A Paradigm for Social Work Practice with People in Poverty. *British Journal of Social Work*, 46(6): 1793–808.

Obasi, C (2022) Black Social Workers: Identity, Racism, Invisibility/Hypervisibility at Work. *Journal of Social Work*, March 2022, 22(2): 479–97.

Olusoga, D (2021) *Black and British: A Forgotten History*. London: Picador.

Phillips, C and Bowling, B (2017) Ethnicities, Racism, Crime, and Criminal Justice. In Liebling, A (ed) *The Oxford Handbook of Criminology* (pp 190–212). Oxford: Oxford University Press.

Priest, N, Paradies, Y, Trenerry, B, Truong, M, Karlsen, S and Kelly, Y (2013) A Systematic Review of Studies Examining the Relationship between Reported Racism and Health and Well-being for Children and Young People. *Social Science and Medicine*, 95(October 2013): 115–27.

Sewell, T et al (2021) Commission on Race and Ethnic Disparities. Available at: https://assets.publishing.service.gov.uk/media/6062ddb1d3bf7f5ce1 060aa4/20210331_-_CRED_Report_-_FINAL_-_Web_Accessible.pdf (accessed 7 January 2025).

Social Work England Professional Standards (2019) Available at: www.socialworkengland.org.uk/standards/professional-standards/ (accessed 7 January 2025).

We are Citizens Advice (2023) Is the 'Cost of Living' a Racial Crisis? Available at: https://wearecitizensadvice.org.uk/is-the-cost-of-living-a-racial-crisis-39090d85e428 (accessed 7 January 2025).

CHAPTER 4

ANTI-RACIST LEARNING FROM FAMILY GROUP CONFERENCING WITH RACIALLY MINORITISED FAMILIES

Omar Mohamed

Introduction

This chapter examines the potential for anti-racism in Family Group Conferencing (FGC) with racially minoritised families and considers what this might mean for social work. To do this, it draws on the systematic literature review I completed as part of my Bachelors in Social Work dissertation (Mohamed, 2023). The literature suggests racially minoritised families find FGC to be empowering and that at times, it meets their cultural needs. But we need to be curious about how culturally adaptable FGC is for racially minoritised communities in the United Kingdom.

FGC is a model of mediated family-led planning in which an FGC trained coordinator supports a family network to work together as a group to make decisions to resolve the difficulties being experienced. FGC's values and principles are about family participation. The model has been operating in the UK since 1991 but it originated in New Zealand where it was developed to enable Māori values and culture shape and underpin work between social workers and Māori communities. FGC aligns well with social work values by creating a safe space for families to develop autonomy, participation and redistribution of power imbalances. It can be presented as an indigenous model of engaging with family networks and it's relevant for social workers working with racially minoritised communities in England. I think FGC also aligns with aims of decolonisation, cultural competence and anti-racist practice as it argues for the need to explore how indigenous knowledge can be valued more effectively in local and global social work practice.

There's a wide body of research to give more detail into how FGC operates in practice, but this chapter discusses its key learning points for anti-racism.

FGC coordinators: their skills, abilities and approaches

The literature emphasises the skills and approaches of FGC coordinators and shows what we can learn from these. The importance of cultural competence, effective use of interpreters and the value of bilingual and racially diverse FGC coordinators and social workers is highlighted. The matching of families with coordinators from the same cultural background is usually seen to be preferable as many racially minoritised cultures in England would typically look to elders, older adults or other respected members of the community to support difficulties and assist in decision making. But matching coordinators is neither always possible nor always desirable, as some communities would reject the idea of having a coordinator from the same background and would see this as a shameful invasion of their privacy within the community.

Shame and stigma can be particularly powerful among some cultures, and this is a helpful example of how we should avoid generalising the way different communities might perceive family or professional involvements. Coordinators, like social workers, regardless of their own cultural backgrounds, need the ability to work cross-culturally, to reflect on their own cultural context and history and to have a clear understanding of racism and anti-oppressive practice. To facilitate the involvement of others in the community, coordinators must be committed to understanding culturally specific issues and to the application of culture within individual families and communities.

Coordinators play an integral role in preparing and encouraging families to engage in the FGC process and where they're trained in cultural differences and have the skills to understand issues of ethnicity and cultural contexts, there are more likely to be positive outcomes.

FGC process: applicability, adequacy and appropriateness

The literature suggests FGC is seen as most respectful where it actively engages with the family's culture and prioritises the voice of the family over the voice of the professional. FGC enables services to respond in a culturally appropriate way because it respects cultural practices, locates ownership of a family's matters within the family and mitigates oppressive power imbalances such as social workers affording more value to their own knowledge and understanding than the family's. FGC can also promote children's rights to cultural belonging and family interdependence by ensuring placements are consistent with principles rooted in the values of the family. Such principles are often referred to as indigenous values.

It's agreed in the literature that FGC enhances the ability to undertake culturally adequate and appropriate social work but barriers to achieving this are also explored. FGC demands significant time for preparatory work, and deep understanding of the traditional values of FGC. These are rooted in Māori culture and include the promotion of empowerment, equity in decision making and respect for diversity. Racially minoritised families may have experienced a loss of family networks due to migration. There may be an unfamiliarity with Western systems, and often racism and discrimination prohibits racially minoritised families from accessing FGCs. Other barriers include the difficulty in matching coordinators from the same ethnic background to the family, difficulty in accessing translation, and issues about confidentiality with different family dynamics within a community.

The literature considers the importance of location, space and environment as significant factors in improving engagement and outcomes for racially minoritised families. It may, for example, be helpful for the FGC to be held in the home of a respected relative. But it's important to not make assumptions as different cultural understandings of power could lead to younger family members not being effectively heard.

When planning to work with a family, it's helpful to:

- research relevant cultural norms within the family network;
- develop insights into the community and family approaches;

- establish how to meet language needs, and

- ensure practical planning for the venue such as appropriate:

  - food choices;

  - music;

  - religious observance;

  - cultural greetings and

  - the geographical and cultural space in which the FGC takes place.

All these considerations should be extended to Gypsy, Roma and Traveller families and to Jewish families, and recognition should be given to the difference in cultural principles and practices that can otherwise be overlooked.

FGC and cultural competence: cultural consultancy and community engagement

FGC coordinators develop cultural competence through the perspective of community-based service providers and workers. Cultural competence is often seen as the respect, honour and understanding for different values, beliefs and ways of being. It's also the inclusion of this understanding into our practice and policy. Development of such understanding and insight is a skill, and one can never become truly 'competent' in cultures different to our own. Social workers might consider a position of 'cultural humility' to be more appropriate and it's helpful for us to reflect on how responsive we are to cultural diversity.

The literature positions culture as the 'central notion'; it's the sum of life patterns passed on throughout generations which includes language, religious ideals, habits of thinking, artistic expression and patterns of social and interpersonal relationships (Lum, 1999, p 2). The literature explores how professionals involved in FGC understand and utilise culture and why this is important. Multiple studies explore the notions of 'cultural consultancy' and community engagement as this is seen as critical in work with marginalised groups and communities and is inherently consistent with anti-oppressive practice and social work values. Cultural consultancy is where coordinators and social workers approach other cultural brokers and organisations for further knowledge and understanding about their culture. Cultural consultants might include steering groups that involve racially minoritised communities, religious organisations and institutions, community outreach groups, educational programmes and any community groups sharing understanding about their culture. Working with cultural consultants demands skill and commitment to partnership working and this requires meaningful groundwork such as approaching organisations with humility and wanting to learn more about culture with the values of being respectful, non-judgemental and open-minded. This helps create meaningful relationships with community-based organisations. Where successful, this can offer important and more nuanced understandings of the community.

Not surprisingly, the literature suggests that such activity brings benefits for racially minoritised families engaging with FGC, but the literature also pinpoints the lack of time available for professionals to undertake this important outreach and collaborative work. This difficulty may be exacerbated by the hesitance and resistance community organisations might have in engaging with statutory services.

FGC and decolonisation: challenging Westernism and Eurocentrism

I've previously spoken about the drive to decolonise social work through challenging the promotion of prevalently Western and Eurocentric practice models (Katoto et al, 2022). The involvement of extended families in dealing with problems is a step away from more traditional Western approaches to problem solving and shows congruency with minoritised cultures and the adoption of similar methods of problem solving throughout their culture for generations. Distrust has led to racially minoritised families being generally not keen on engaging with 'White organisations' such as social services. So when an FGC is conducted in the family's own language and translated into English for the professionals, families are likely to feel more comfortable as it's the professionals who are expected to adapt rather than the family.

FGC moves away from interventions that are typically rooted in colonialist ideas. By resisting 'White organisations' and Western models of social work,

Māori cultural traditions were able to contribute to models of problem solving that fit the cultural contexts of racially minoritised families. Family-orientated and person-centred practice is generally considered more appropriate for practitioners working with racially minoritised families as these families typically rely on family resources as part of their cultural understandings and practices.

CASE STORY

Imagine you are working as a children and families social worker with two teenage children of mixed heritage. Their mother has mixed Black Caribbean and Irish Traveller heritage and their father is Black Caribbean. The maternal family network are significant relationships for the family. The children have been permanently excluded from school, the father is in prison for assault and the mother has a diagnosis of ADHD and depression.

A referral has come in from the school to suggest the mother is unable to keep her children safe. There are concerns that the children have been selling drugs in school and getting involved in fights. The mother has historically refused support from family support workers and social workers due to the distrust of services.

A family group conference is suggested. The mother reluctantly accepts this on the understanding that it can be held at her own mother's home, that it will be with her friends, neighbours and an anti-racist advocate instead of social work professionals and that ackee and saltfish will be served. These suggestions have been discussed between the social worker, FGC coordinator and the mother.

The FGC discussion focuses particularly on the impact of racism on the family and on the mother's fight for her own diagnosis as well as for recognition of her children's potential neurodiversity. It also reflects on the impact on the family of the father having been incarcerated for an assault where he was protecting the mother and the children were being punished for having difficulties at school as well as potential criminal exploitation. This conversation links to the maternal grandmother's perspective of being part of the Windrush generation, her experiences of institutional racism, and the way in which these themes could be identified across the ancestry.

A plan is offered to social services to work in a way that recognises how institutional and systemic racism impacts the family, and acknowledges the need to address, empower and advocate around these issues for the family to make the changes it would like to see. Specifically, the plan requests that the allocated social worker makes a statement to the family to recognise the impact of racism on the experiences of the family and that the social worker supports the mother to write a letter to the children's school to explore the potential unconscious bias and challenge the decision to exclude the children from the school.

Conclusion

This chapter has reflected on the benefits of learning from FGC for social workers who wish to practise in an anti-racist way. By engaging with indigenous models of working with people, it has built on key principles of respect and value for cultural diversity, working with people and communities to shift power dynamics, and ultimately addressing the impact that racism and colonialisation has had on how we practise as social workers.

Reflective questions to move us forward

1. How can we support social workers and FGC coordinators from an ethnic or racial diasporic community to share their diasporic, indigenous and/or ancestral knowledge?

2. How do we promote and develop cultural humility, consultancy and responsiveness as skills that need ongoing work?

3. How could you incorporate questions about family stories in your work with families? Consider asking about how ancestors might have resolved issues in the family.

References

Katoto, D, Mohamed, O and Moore, T (2022) The Road to Activism. In Moore, T and Simango, G (eds) *The Anti-Racist Social Worker: Stories of Activism in Social Care and Allied Health Professionals*. St Albans: Critical Publishing.

Lum, D (1999) *Culturally Competent Practice: A Framework for Growth and Action*. Pacific Grove, CA: Brooks/Cole Publishing Company.

Mohamed, O (2023) A Systematic Literature Review with Racially Minoritised People Using Family Group Conferencing in England. *Practice*, 36(1): 19–37. https://doi.org/10.1080/09503153.2023.2234102.

CHAPTER 5

TRANSFORMATIVE PRACTICE IN THE CRIMINAL JUSTICE SYSTEM

Kristel Campbell-Bobb

Introduction

As a social worker deeply entrenched in the UK's Youth Justice System (YJS), my commitment to anti-racism is both a professional duty and a personal mission. Growing up in a multicultural environment, I witnessed stark disparities in how different racial groups were treated. These experiences fuelled my passion for social justice and informed my understanding of the pervasive nature of systemic racism.

Social workers within the YJS are at the forefront of addressing the needs of marginalised young people. This means we can advocate for systemic changes to address racial inequalities. In my work within the YJS, I've encountered young people whose lives have been profoundly affected by racial bias and discrimination. This has reinforced my belief that social workers must challenge and dismantle this injustice. Anti-racism is not an abstract concept but a practical necessity that should shape how we approach every aspect of our work, from direct practice to influencing policy and advocating for systemic change. My journey into social work was driven by a desire to make a difference in the lives of young people, particularly those from marginalised communities. Early in my career, I realised that racist systemic barriers perpetuate cycles of disadvantage and criminalisation. Witnessing this first-hand reinforced my commitment to anti-racist practice.

This chapter is about the importance of critical reflection to recognise racial bias in practice. I share an (anonymised) case story and introduce my own TRUE model of reflection to show how it supports my endeavours to be an anti-racist social worker.

Critical social work is rooted in a deep understanding of power dynamics and oppressions. It challenges racist barriers and structures and promotes social justice (Dominelli, 2002). It also recognises the significance of contextual factors in people's lives and highlights the pivotal role social workers play in advocating for change (Fook, 2002). It's explicitly committed to advancing greater social justice and equality for those who are oppressed and marginalised in society (Allan, 2009).

Critical social work provides a valuable framework for addressing the complex and interconnected issues faced by young people in the YJS. Its understanding that social problems are often rooted in inequality encourages social workers to look beyond individual behaviour and consider the broader context. Promoting equity and justice within the YJS demands a commitment to anti-racist principles and the challenge of discriminatory practices and policies. As social workers, we advocate for fair treatment for marginalised young people. This includes access to education, employment and housing as well as support for good mental health. But we must also push for policy changes that reflect the experiences of those most affected by systemic inequalities. By doing so, we can help create a more just and humane YJS that supports all young people's well-being and development.

The intensity of daily pressures faced by social workers can lead to focus on crisis management at the expense of understanding the broader context (Maclean, 2020). This shift in view can contribute to issues like adultification (imposition of adult sensibilities onto a child) and disproportionality (over or under-representation of a particular group compared to its proportion in the general population). These issues can be exacerbated by emphasis on efficiency, which can lead to loss of focus on the child.

Core to our response to these pressures is critical reflection. This is a cornerstone of anti-racist practice which asks us to examine our own biases and influences, to question the assumptions underlying our practice and to be open to different perspectives. Critical reflection helps us better understand the impact of racism and develop more equitable approaches to intervention. It embraces uncomfortable conversations as drivers for personal growth and invites open, challenging discussion to underpin anti-racist practice. Just as active listening and empathetic conversations build trust with clients, colleagues and communities, so genuine understanding of diverse perspectives can create inclusive environments and dismantling of stereotypes and discriminatory practices in the criminal justice system.

I created the 'TRUE' model of reflection to facilitate my own critical reflection (see Figure 5.1). 'TRUE' is an acronym for:

- **T** – **Time** needed for reflection;

- **R** – **Realisation** of new awareness **and Recognition** of patterns/trends/behaviours;

- **U** – **Understanding** and linking to broader principles and learning;

- **E** – **Enhancement** of future practice.

The model asks us to identify a 'Point of Reflection', for example, a dilemma, thought or feeling. Then, it offers six options for focus. These are (i) Feelings and emotions, (ii) Power dynamics, (iii) Values, (iv) Knowledge, (v) Self-awareness and (vi) Uncertainty. I suggest reflection on each of these areas offers an effective platform for insight that can lead to useful change. Further prompts guide our reflection and invite us to consider our dilemma through the lens of the Social GGRRAAACCEEESSS:

• *Gender*	• *Ability*	• *Ethnicity*
• *Geography*	• *Appearance*	• *Economics*
• *Race*	• *Culture*	• *Spirituality*
• *Religion*	• *Class/Caste*	• *Sexuality*
• *Age*	• *Education*	• *Sexual orientation*
		(Burnham, 2012)

THE T.R.U.E MODEL OF REFLECTION

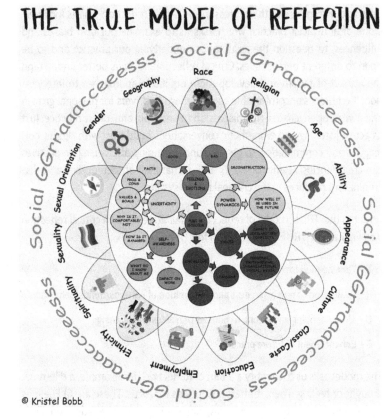

© Kristel Bobb

Figure 5.1 The TRUE model of reflection (Campbell-Bobb, 2022)

CASE STORY

Demonstrating anti-racism in practice

Consider the case of Jamal, a 16 year-old Black boy living in a deprived urban neighbourhood with high levels of gang activity. Jamal had several run-ins with the law, primarily related to minor drug offences and suspected gang involvement. Traditionally, such cases might be approached with a focus on punishment, reinforcing negative stereotypes about Black youth and perpetuating cycles of marginalisation and criminalisation. But the TRUE model of reflection guides us towards an anti-racist response to Jamal's situation.

TRUE model of reflection

The point of reflection identified is 'how to respond to Jamal's offending behaviour?'.

The beauty of the TRUE model of reflection is the extent to which it can be used. The following example holds Jamal's ethnicity in mind, but one can then progress to consider the six areas of focus along with any and/or all the other Social GGRRRAAACCEEESSS:

- **Knowledge**

  What do I know about Jamal's ethnicity? What is fact and what do I need to learn?

- **Values**

  What similarities/differences are there in my personal, professional, organisational, social, wider media, local values to Jamal's and how do I consider his ethnicity to impact these similarities or differences in values?

$\longrightarrow$

- **Power dynamics**

  What impact do power dynamics have on my decision making? Who is holding the power and why? Where does ethnicity position Jamal in terms of power? How can this power be used to inform this decision?

- **Feelings and emotions**

  What are my (brutally!) honest negative feelings about Jamal? Why do I feel that? What are my positive feelings about Jamal and why?

- **Self-awareness**

  What do I know about me? Can I jump to conclusions? How do my personal experiences or assumptions impact my decision making? Eg Am I in a more privileged position and am I considering that privilege in my decision making?

- **Uncertainty**

  What are the facts? What do we know for certain and what are the possibilities? What are the positive/negative aspects of these considered uncertainties? How do these fit with Jamal's values and goals and how do these compare with mine? What exactly is it that makes me feel comfortable/uncomfortable about uncertainty? How am I managing my feelings about the present uncertainty?

As Jamal's social worker, application of the TRUE model of reflection empowers me to challenge the stereotype that young Black males are inherently more prone to criminal behaviour (**Knowledge**). Instead, I recognise that Jamal's actions were influenced by a range of social determinants, including his living conditions, exposure to violence and limited access to positive opportunities (**Uncertainty**). By reflecting on these factors, I'm able to develop a more nuanced understanding of Jamal's situation and tailor my interventions accordingly.

In Jamal's situation, my approach involved understanding of Contextual Safeguarding (Firmin, 2017) which recognises that young people are often influenced by their environment and addresses the broader social and community factors that contribute to criminal behaviour (***Self-Awareness –*** *comparison of Jamal's experiences to my own and the impact any similarities or differences might have on my decision making*). The TRUE model helped me focus on geography and location and to consider the more local context dynamics and how these impact on Jamal (***Values***). This led me to explore in which localities he could feel safe and to identify his positive role models. We were then able to create a safer and more supportive environment for Jamal. Central to this was Jamal having alternative strategies to avoid risk, protect himself and to know what to do and who to contact if he didn't feel safe (***Feelings and Emotions***). This helped him reduce his involvement in criminal activities and also provided him with the resources and opportunities he needed to succeed.

Advocacy is a critical component of anti-racist practice, as it involves challenging the systemic inequalities that perpetuate racial disparities within the criminal justice system. Considering ***Power Dynamics*** for Jamal meant working closely with his legal team to ensure he received fair treatment and highlighting the mitigating circumstances of his situation. It also involved pushing for changes within the YJS to address the broader issues of racial bias and discrimination. By advocating for Jamal's rights and challenging discriminatory practices, I ensured Jamal received the support he needed to rebuild his life and avoid future involvement in the criminal justice system.

The TRUE model of reflection encourages me to take the Time to reflect, to Recognise patterns and see where Jamal enjoys and excels, to Understand the dynamics and influencing factors to behaviours and to Enhance my practice by applying the insights gained to improve my support for Jamal. This has meant focusing on his strengths and providing him with opportunities for personal development. By engaging him in mentorship programmes and skills training, I could help Jamal build a positive future and develop the confidence and resilience he needed to overcome the challenges he faced.

Integrating anti-racist principles into everyday practice involves a commitment to continuous learning and growth. This means actively seeking out opportunities to engage in critical reflection and dialogue to develop a deeper understanding of the issues faced by marginalised communities. It helps us to be more culturally responsive and tailored to the unique needs of each individual.

Anti-racism in the YJS is an ongoing effort. By critically examining personal biases, advocating for systemic change and empowering marginalised youth, we can create a more just and equitable criminal justice system. TRUE reflection on our experiences deepens our understanding of systemic racism and empowers us to advocate for better.

TRUE has become a key aspect of my anti-racist practice, as it helps me recognise and respond to the cycles of marginalisation and criminalisation by providing young people with the tools and support they need to succeed. I hope readers find it similarly helpful in their own effort to eliminate racial biases in practice.

Reflective questions to move us forward

1. How do your personal experiences and biases influence your interactions with young people from diverse racial backgrounds in the YJS?

2. In what ways can you leverage your position as a social worker to advocate for systemic changes that address racial inequalities within the criminal justice system?

3. How might the TRUE model of reflection help you integrate anti-racist principles into everyday practice?

References

Allan, J (2009) *Critical Social Work: Theories and Practices for a Socially Just World*. London: Taylor & Francis Group.

Burnham, J (2012) Developments in Social GGRRAAACCEEESSS: Visible-Invisible and Voiced-Unvoiced. In Krause, I (ed) *Culture and Reflexivity in Systemic Psychotherapy: Mutual Perspectives* (pp 139–60). London: Karnac Books.

Dominelli, L (2002) *Anti-Oppressive Social Work Theory and Practice*. Basingstoke: Palgrave Macmillan.

Firmin, C (2017) Contextual Risk, Individualised Responses: An Assessment of Safeguarding Responses to Nine Cases of Peer-on-Peer Abuse. *Child Abuse Review*, 27(1): 42–57. doi: 10.1002/car.2449.

Fook, J (2002) *Social Work: Critical Theory and Practice*. London: Sage Publications.

Maclean, S (2020) What/Why? How? A Simple Framework for Social Work Practice. YouTube. Available at: www.youtube.com/watch?v=1YD8rdKqOUk (accessed 15 February 2025).

CHAPTER 6

A FOSTER CARER'S PERSPECTIVE: ALLYSHIP AND ADVOCACY IN THE FACE OF DISCRIMINATION

Narges Qauyumi

Introduction

For a long time, I lived under the illusion that I had never experienced discrimination or racial inequality. It was when I began my practice in social work that I realised I had developed a skill for removing myself from uncomfortable conversations and environments before discussions about my race would begin. I mastered a way of hiding in between my South Asian British self and my travelled accent which unavoidably comes up in any new interaction I make. I mastered a skill of shutting down the narrative of poor Afghans versus Talibans by sharing its history and intellectualising the conversation, moving away from the fact that I came into this country as an immigrant seeking asylum and disregarding the parts of me that identify as a Muslim woman, albeit a part-time Muslim. But what happens when after four years of mainstream fostering with my local authority, caring for a total of six teenage children aged between 12 and 18, I was put forward for deregistration due to my religious practices and beliefs?

This happened because my newly allocated supervising social worker considered my refusal to allow young people to bring non-halal meat into our home to be an issue. It was recorded in our 'Form F' fostering assessment that we would instead cater for our foster children's wider choices by taking them out to restaurants. But now I was expected, as a Muslim carer, to allow non-halal meat in my fostering household. How could I avoid this part of my Muslimness?

Reflections

While my journey may seem surreal, I have come to realise that my own lived experience is alarmingly more common than we might think. Not everyone has found the courage to share their experiences and have instead found themselves silenced through shame. I hope my story provides my readers with a reality check on our own biases and our individual journeys through the complex nuances of racism in everyday life.

In Islam, following halal principles is a religious obligation that ensures the preservation of one's religious integrity through dietary choices. The Qur'an emphasises the importance of this. The crucial point here is that if I wanted to continue to be a foster carer, I had to go against my religious beliefs and practice. Because I actively challenged this, the matter escalated to the point of deregistration, with the claim that I was no longer meeting the National Minimum Fostering Standards (Department of Education, 2011).

Growing up in care – a varied experience for all of us – often felt, and sometimes still feels, as though I am not seen, heard or valued. To me, providing a safe space means being able to tell my story and unapologetically putting my name to it for others to see, read and hear. I am fully aware that this topic of discussion is highly sensitive. I am also mindful that I represent the voice of not only many Muslim foster carers, but also care experienced people who have shared lived experiences of racial discrimination. This makes this chapter even more important to me.

Uncovering allyship

The power of allyship is by far the most underestimated concept – easily explained, yet not often seen to have much value. Let me tell you how my allies supported me.

As an independent fostering panel advisor, I have overseen deregistration of foster carers in a professional capacity. My own experience of deregistration as a foster carer made me feel as though part of my identity was being stripped away. As a care experienced social worker, a mainstream foster carer and a kinship carer, caring was and continues to be at the core of my identity. The deregistration process dragged on for two years before concluding. It made me feel like an imposter, a fraud in every part of my life. Despite working in the world of social care, I felt rejected. Was the care I provided not good enough because my belief system did not align with how I was asked to practise?

In the beginning, I hid my story from all but one Muslim foster carer. They validated my experience and highlighted that my battle was for all Muslim foster carers. I was constantly reminded, *'If social care could treat one of their own like this, then what would happen to the rest of us Muslim carers, who don't have the same footing as you?'* They recognised this was a heavy burden to carry alone. There would have been no shame had I chosen to walk away.

Allyship, in this case, was about validation, reflection and recognition of a larger struggle. It made me realise how helpful it might have been had I been provided with such a space with my supervising social worker. Unfortunately, I felt my worker at the time was out of her depth. I was met with silence and directed to speak to managers instead. We aren't experts, and there's no shame in not knowing how to approach a new challenge, but it would have been helpful if my worker had asked me more questions about my beliefs and values and helped me to align these with the fostering standards, which, let's be clear, are open to interpretation.

Lastly, a note to self: it would have been helpful if I hadn't met fear with fear. I recognised this much later in my journey. Of course, I was challenging, but as, with support from my allies, I grew confident in my stance, I could see there was no existing policy to guide practice on this, and it was from here that both mine and my supervising social worker's fears stemmed.

The internal dialogue of whether to walk away or stay and see this journey through became more complicated and difficult when my social work registration was at risk of being diminished. I made the conscious decision to inform my work managers, who sought advice from the Local Authority Designated Officer (LADO). This is the person who is notified when it has been alleged that someone working with children has behaved in a way that has harmed or may harm a child. Words cannot adequately describe the dread I felt in the days that followed.

My manager sought advice through his service manager and the LADO. He spoke to my fostering local authority to understand their challenges and concerns. His insistence on understanding more before forming his own views exemplified allyship and affirmed his stance supporting anti-racist practice. He provided a positive reference for me to share with the fostering panel. He was not afraid to voice his views and professional opinion of me as a social worker although this differed starkly from the narrative offered by the fostering team. This was the deciding moment for me – where I chose to stay and see this battle through to the end.

Seeking courage

I reflected on the courage my scrawny 16 year-old self had when I admitted myself into care. I was standing up against my abuse. I was yearning for change and to be treated with basic dignity and respect. That courage was innate; I was fearless, going against my culture, my family, and breaking free from being silent. Now I was desperately seeking that little girl's courage, a part of me I knew still existed.

I found pockets of anti-racist practice in care experienced organisations. It's in the way they create space for people with lived experience to play a part in the delivery of training and practice within fostering and adoption panels. It's in Muslim-specific fostering organisations, in their motivation to break down barriers faced through the recruitment of Muslim foster carers and adoptees. It's in fostering resources, in their drive to enable foster carers to navigate their rights by breaking down systems, policy and legislation. It's in fostering panels, in holding a reflective and non-judgemental space for all their contributing members. And it's in the Foster Carers Union; for their fearless take in fighting for the rights of their carers through employment tribunals.

Reflecting on the recruitment drive for more diverse foster carers and looking at the barriers around hard-to-reach groups, it would be helpful for local authorities to create toolkits that empower foster carers to practise alongside their religious beliefs. For example, local authorities could utilise their existing diverse carers to co-produce practice guides to support carers and professionals to navigate and address challenges around halal and non-halal foods. Another example could be the Mockingbird Family Model (2024). This creates a support network similar to that of an extended family for foster carers, providing children and their carers with support. This approach places families at the centre of solutions and problem solving. It uses restorative approaches to ensure placement stability for looked after children.

It was helpful when my Fostering Network advisor directed me to my own existing toolkit which was my knowledge and skills as a social worker. They encouraged me to write my own report and present a formal response to the local authority's report.

My advisor presented professional curiosity in wanting to know and understand my lived experience. Their skilful questioning allowed me to step away from the victim narrative and channel my anger and frustration into reflection. This allowed me to see the element of resistance on my part that prevented me from addressing the challenges at hand. This clarity of thought allowed me to evoke and spark panel members to think beyond the narrative presented to them.

Concluding thoughts

Racial disparity, at least in my experience, is not as simple as Black versus White. For instance, during my deregistration process, I had Pakistani, Indian and African Caribbean managers overseeing my case.

Admirably, my new supervising social worker was not afraid to challenge the local authority she represented. She upheld her social work values and practised these standards by challenging the recommendation for my deregistration, and my approval to continue fostering was reinstated by panel members.

The support and allyship I received on this journey came from people of all walks of life. The point here is that colour does not exclude anyone from being racist or having conscious and unconscious biases towards any group of people. In the same way, colour does not exempt anyone from experiencing discrimination and alienation.

In closing, I want my readers to understand we are the creators of our own toolkit and are capable of helping ourselves out of any dilemma that requires us to challenge racial abuse. The journey is long, tiring and often exhausting. Recognition that the fight is much larger than any individual can feel overwhelming. It may seem like one voice or narrative won't make a significant impact, but this is far from the truth.

To be fearless, we must embrace allyship by sharing our experiences. We must build courage by seeking support and we must continue to strengthen our knowledge, skills and practice. By doing so, we contribute to a collective effort that makes a powerful impact, proving that every voice and every narrative matters in the fight against racial discrimination.

Reflective questions to move us forward

1. In your own journey through anti-racist practice, what impact do you think you've had as an ally in combatting covert or overt experiences of racist practice?

2. Is it enough to meet diversity quotas through new hires? Does this truly support diversity beyond numbers? Hopefully, you've answered no to both of those questions. Now I want you to really reflect: how can we create an inclusive environment where existing diverse carers feel valued and empowered to advance?

3. I am curious to know, how might you have practised professional curiosity in this instance, setting aside your own ego (obviously)?

References

Department of Education (2011) Fostering Services: National Minimum Standards. London. Available at: www.gov.uk/government/publications/fostering-services-national-minimum-standards (accessed 9 January 2025).

The Mockingbird Society (2024) https://mockingbirdsociety.org/our-work/mockingbird-family (accessed 9 January 2025).

CHAPTER 7

BREAKING CHAINS AND BUILDING BRIDGES: A JOURNEY TOWARDS ANTI-RACIST PRACTICE

Clenton Farquharson

Introduction

This chapter sets out a journey to become better and fairer social workers.

Social workers are people who help those in need, often the most marginalised in our society.

We learn from a story about someone who has worked with social workers and really knows their world.

We look closely at this story to see what made things better and what made things worse, especially focusing on racism and exclusion.

By understanding these details, we want to figure out how social workers can either help make things better or unintentionally worsen these issues.

But understanding isn't enough; we need to take action.

We explore creative and innovative ways to get rid of bias, which means any unfair treatment, in how we help and support people.

This means making sure our methods are welcoming to everyone, regardless of their background, and reflect the diverse society we live in, especially in the UK.

This chapter is a call to all social workers to think deeply about their actions, keep learning and strive to improve.

We need to rethink how we work to better support and lift up everyone we serve.

By doing this, we aim to break down the barriers that keep some people from getting the help and support they need, and create a fairer society.

Through this journey, we hope to inspire a strong commitment to social justice, making it a key part of our everyday actions and decisions.

It's about making sure everyone is treated fairly and with respect, all the time.

My relationship to anti-racism in social work

I'm a Black Disabled Man who draws on the services of social workers. Because of this, I've seen how crucial it is for social workers to fight against racism. Living with these identities has shown me the barriers and unfair treatment people can face because of their race or disability. These experiences have made me passionate about social justice, which means fair treatment for everyone.

Growing up, I saw a lot of unfairness and bias. When I needed help from social workers, they often didn't understand my unique challenges. They might have meant well, but they didn't always get what it was like to live with both racial prejudice and a disability. This made things harder for me and others like me.

These experiences taught me how important it is for social workers to break the chains of racism and ableism (discrimination against disabled people). This means getting rid of unfair treatment and building bridges of understanding and support. Social workers need to understand and respect the different backgrounds and challenges of the people they help.

Seeing the struggles of others and myself because of racial prejudice made me want to advocate for social justice. I believe everyone should be treated fairly and with respect, no matter who they are. By sharing my story, I hope to show why it's important for social workers to be aware of and fight against racism and ableism. It's about making sure everyone, regardless of their race or disability, gets the support and understanding they need to live their best lives.

Why anti-racism matters in social work

In social work, being anti-racist isn't just a nice idea; it's something we absolutely need to do.

It means recognising and dealing with unfair biases and systems that hurt people.

As someone who has used social worker services, I've seen firsthand how important it is to break the chains of discrimination and build bridges of empathy and support.

This focus on breaking chains and building bridges is key to making sure our work is fair and includes everyone.

CASE STORY

A personal reflection: story of practice

In my career, I've worked with people from many different backgrounds.

These experiences have shown me how important it is to adopt an anti-racist approach in social work.

Let me tell you about Ahmed, a young man from Syria.

$\rightarrow$

Ahmed faced many challenges when he came here, like language barriers, getting used to a new culture and facing discrimination.

His experience with social workers was mixed.

Some social workers were really supportive, but others had biases that affected the quality of help he received.

For example, one social worker might have assumed things about Ahmed based on his background, making it harder for him to get the best support.

My goal was to ensure Ahmed felt supported, heard and valued.

I wanted to break the chains of prejudice and build bridges of trust and understanding with him.

By doing this, I aimed to show Ahmed that he could rely on social workers and that they respected his experiences and needs.

This meant actively listening to him, understanding his cultural background and fighting against any biases that might get in the way of providing the best help possible.

In working with Ahmed, I learned about the significance of hospitality and communal support in Syrian culture, which influenced me to involve his local Syrian community in his support network. This enhanced his sense of belonging, built trust and ensured the support he received was respectful and effective.

This approach can make a huge difference in someone's life, helping them feel more included and supported.

Discussing the story

Recognising bias and privilege

To become better social workers, we first need to recognise our own biases (unfair thoughts) and privileges (advantages we have).

This means taking a close look at our beliefs and experiences to understand how they affect the way we treat others.

By understanding these influences, we can break the chains of prejudice and build bridges towards more inclusive support.

Let's break it down. Biases are like hidden opinions or stereotypes we might have about people based on things like their race, gender or background.

Privileges are the advantages we might have because of who we are, like being treated better because of our skin colour or social status.

Recognising these is important because they can shape how we interact with others, often in ways we don't even realise.

In my work with Ahmed, a young man from Syria, I made a promise to myself to constantly check my own assumptions and privileges.

For example, I would ask myself if I was making any assumptions about him just because he's from a different country or has a different culture.

This kind of self-reflection is something I do all the time, not just once.

By doing this, I try to create a more inclusive and empathetic environment.

This means making sure everyone feels understood and respected, and actively fighting against all forms of racism.

It's about making sure our support is fair and welcoming to everyone, regardless of their background.

This ongoing effort helps us be better social workers and build stronger, more trusting relationships with the people we help.

Building trust and cultural competence

Trust is super important for being a better, anti-racist social worker.

It helps social workers connect better with the people they help.

When I worked with Ahmed, I built trust by really listening to him, acknowledging his experiences and showing genuine empathy.

This made Ahmed feel valued and understood, creating a safe space for him to open up.

Cultural competence means understanding and respecting the cultural background, values and beliefs of the people we help.

For Ahmed, I took the time to learn about his culture, which is very different from mine.

This meant understanding things like his traditions, customs and the challenges he faced coming from Syria.

By doing this, I made sure my support was sensitive to his needs.

This approach helps break the chains of cultural misunderstanding.

When social workers don't take the time to understand someone's culture, it can lead to mistakes and make people feel misunderstood or unsupported.

But when we learn about and respect different cultures, we build bridges of cultural competence.

This means we can provide better, more effective help and make sure everyone feels respected and valued.

This is key to being a fair and supportive social worker.

Challenging structural inequalities

Fighting racism isn't just about helping individual people; it's also about changing unfair systems in society.

While helping one person at a time is important, it's not enough by itself.

To make lasting changes, I work with community organisations and push for better policies.

This means teaming up with groups that are also trying to fight racism and speaking up to change rules and laws that are unfair.

For example, if there's a law or a rule that makes it harder for certain groups of people to get jobs or good education, I advocate to change that.

By working with others, we can make bigger changes that help everyone, not just one person at a time.

This kind of work helps break the chains of systemic injustice, which are the big, deep-rooted problems that keep unfairness going in our society.

By addressing these larger issues, we build bridges to a fairer society where everyone has equal opportunities and treatment.

So, fighting racism involves both helping individuals and making big changes to the systems that affect us all. This way, we can create a world that's fairer and more just for everyone.

Conclusion

Becoming anti-racist social workers, as shown through my story, requires a strong commitment to self-reflection, learning and growth. This journey isn't about reaching a final destination; it's about constantly becoming more aware, empathetic and effective in our work.

First, we need to look at our own biases – those unfair thoughts we might not even realise we have.

By understanding how these biases affect our behaviour, we can start to change and become better at supporting others.

Building trust with the people we help is crucial.

This means really listening to them, respecting their experiences and showing that we care.

When people feel understood and valued, they are more likely to trust us.

Next, embracing cultural humility and attempt at understanding is important.

This means understanding and respecting the diverse backgrounds, values and beliefs of the people we help.

Everyone is different, and these differences should be valued.

Learning about someone's culture helps us provide better and more sensitive support.

It breaks down misunderstandings and builds connections.

Challenging structural inequalities is another critical part of anti-racist social work.

It's not enough to just help individuals; we also need to address the larger systems that keep unfairness alive.

This means identifying and tackling the barriers that create inequality.

For example, if certain groups of people have a harder time getting jobs or education because of systemic racism, we need to work to change those systems.

This often requires collaborating with community members, other professionals and policymakers to create lasting change.

Facing these issues can be uncomfortable.

We have to confront truths about ourselves and the systems we work in that might not be pleasant.

But it's necessary if we want to make a real difference.

We need to listen to those affected by racism and use our roles to advocate for change.

By doing this, we can help break the chains of oppression and build bridges towards a just and equitable society.

Inspired by creativity and innovation, we must commit to this ongoing journey of anti-racist practice.

Our goal is to make social work a force for positive change in society.

This means constantly finding new and better ways to support everyone, regardless of their background.

Let's hold onto the hope that, through our collective efforts, we can create a world where equality, dignity and justice are not just ideals but realities.

By working together and continually striving to improve, we can help break down barriers and build a society that is fair and welcoming for all.

This ongoing effort is what will ultimately lead to breaking the chains of oppression and building the bridges of a just and equitable society.

Reflective questions to move us forward

Under the headings, ask yourself the following questions.

1. **Self-reflection on bias and privilege:** how do my own biases and privileges shape my interactions with the people I serve, and what steps can I take to continuously recognise and mitigate these influences in my practice?

2. **Cultural humility and trust-building:** in what ways can I deepen my understanding of the diverse cultural backgrounds of people who draw on services to ensure that my support is empathetic,

$\longrightarrow$

respectful and effective? How can I build and maintain trust with individuals who have different experiences and needs from my own?

3. **Addressing structural inequalities**: what specific actions can I take, both individually and in collaboration with others, to challenge and change the systemic inequalities that impact the communities I serve? How can I effectively advocate for policies and practices that promote social justice and equity?

CHAPTER 8

UNVEILING STRENGTH: THE TRANSFORMATIVE POWER OF ANTI-RACISM STORYTELLING – CHANGING THE WORLD ONE STORY AT A TIME

Isaac Samuels

Introduction

In the two decades I've dedicated to adult social care, I've made it my mission to improve people's experiences of this vital sector. But my professional journey has been shaped by personal encounters with racism. These experiences have profoundly influenced my perspective and compelled me to address its impact and to advocate for a more inclusive and supportive social care environment. I've done this using storytelling as a means of change.

As a community campaigner and co-production advisor, I've witnessed firsthand the struggles of people facing disadvantage. My work spans health, social care and housing, and I've been actively engaged in supporting people at risk due to poverty, health conditions, racism, disability and other forms of oppression. My approach is always to make sure people's voices are heard and their experiences valued in the shaping of the policies and practices which directly affect their lives.

My own journey through health and social care has been marked by personal challenges. My experiences of severe and enduring mental health challenges, chronic pain and fatigue due to HIV have guided my efforts to break down the stigma associated with certain conditions and generated a compassionate, rights-based approach in all aspects of my work.

I've been involved in research, practice and co-production in social work, nursing, mental health and HIV stigma. Co-production is central to my philosophy because it means people aren't seen as passive recipients of care but as active participants in defining their own narratives and outcomes. But by advocating anti-racism as integral to co-production, I aim to contribute to a social care system that's fair, compassionate and truly reflective of the diverse needs of those it serves.

Co-production and anti-racism: crafting inclusive narratives

Co-production is a transformative approach that bridges gaps. It weaves together the expertise of stakeholders such as community members, social care providers and policymakers, to tackle complex issues. Its essence lies in collaboration; every voice is valued, and every perspective is integrated into the decision-making process. Co-production fosters innovation and creates solutions that are robust because they're generated from the communities they serve. But co-production also exists within individual relationships. At their best, the relationship between the person and their social worker is a co-production in which they work together to find the best way to achieve change.

Anti-racism is at the heart of effective co-production. It demands intentional effort to confront bias, address power imbalance and create space where diverse perspectives can flourish. Embracing anti-racism ensures all participants – especially those historically marginalised – have equal opportunities to both contribute and benefit.

Within the arena of anti-racist co-production, storytelling and *story listening* is a powerful tool. Stories illuminate the lived realities of ethnically marginalised communities. They highlight the struggles and celebrate the victories. It's through stories that we can create deeper understanding and drive change by transforming abstract concepts into tangible realities. Our collective stories and shared experiences are the foundation upon which a more inclusive and effective co-production model is built. *'Ubuntu: I am because we are'* (traditional African proverb).

As someone who has been harmed by racism in the context of health and social care, for me anti-racism is more than just opposing racism. It's actively challenging and dismantling systemic racial inequities. This is central to co-production, where the aim is for everyone, particularly people with lived experiences who are also racially or ethnically marginalised, to have equal opportunities to contribute and benefit. Anti-racist co-production demands a deliberate effort to confront biases, address power imbalances and create inclusive spaces where diverse voices are heard and valued.

CASE STORY

My storytelling of anti-racist social care

My own story involves David, the social worker who had a profound impact on my life. At that time, my needs as someone from a racialised background were often misunderstood or dismissed. I faced instances of racism that compounded my struggles and left me feeling isolated and disheartened.

David was assigned to me during this particularly tough period, and his approach was refreshingly different. He didn't see me as a 'case' or a set of 'issues' to address; he saw me as a whole person with a multifaceted story. What set David apart was his ability to work with me to co-create a safe and supportive space where I could freely express my experiences. These included the pain and frustration of dealing with racism.

I might now consider this to be an anti-racist, relational co-production that used storytelling to create trust and understanding. But these weren't concepts familiar to me at the time. Certainly, the impact of being able to express my feelings to someone who was actively – and interestedly – listening is one which informs my practice to this day.

Equally as important, David showed up consistently, and not just in the physical sense. It really *felt* as if this wasn't about ticking boxes or

$\rightarrow$

adhering to a rigid framework but rather about David wanting to connect with me on a human level. By valuing my narrative and allowing me to share my experiences in my own words, David helped rebuild my trust in the social work system and was the first social worker who made me feel like he was listening to hear and not to respond.

The first thing David said was, 'Tell me your story'. He wasn't interested in what others had written about me. He wanted to know how I told my story and he actually used these words: 'Tell me your story'. He wasn't asking for my story of accessing services but my story of who I was as a person. David made me feel heard.

My story included (and includes) experiences of racism. David's response was: 'I believe you'. He also said, 'This is painful stuff. Don't shy away from the pain – it's real. Don't stop asking for things to be different; they should be different. Trust in your own intuition and feelings.'

To have this validation from a professional was incredibly affirming and made me feel psychologically and physically safe.

So, what learning can we take from this?

Let's be in no doubt: when someone listens deeply and respects your narrative, without picking it apart or demanding 'evidence', it allows a deep sense of confidence and validation. This experience of empowerment helped me reclaim my strength and navigate my recovery with renewed hope and clarity. David's approach helped me through a difficult period that had been marked by racism. It underscored the profound impact true listening and storytelling can have on personal growth and healing. These interactions have had a lasting and profound effect on me, and I see storytelling as a powerful way to ensure the experiences of racialised people are heard and understood.

Understanding racism

Speaking from my vantage point today, I've realised the work I've done in the last few years is that which my younger self so desperately needed but was unable to articulate. I now recognise that my skills in – and, indeed, commitment to – anti-racist co-production started with my own experience as a 'service user', of having a social worker with whom I was finally able to seek help in dealing with racism as it affected me. David saw me as a whole person with a story that was real and valuable.

Conclusion

Co-production is an important part of social work practice. Anti-racism must be fundamental to this, and storytelling is a powerful way to make this happen.

Storytelling is a cornerstone of anti-racism work because it personalises the complex issues of race and discrimination. The sharing of personal narratives bridges gaps in understanding, amplifies marginalised voices and fosters empathy and connection. Storytelling is an educational tool that reveals the real-life impacts of racism, challenges stereotypes and inspires collective action. It empowers by validating individual experiences and cultural identities, while preserving and celebrating diverse histories. Ultimately, storytelling drives change by building understanding and solidarity in the fight against racism.

Reflective questions to move us forward

1. To what extent is anti-racism a part of your day-to-day work?

2. How can storytelling and story listening help you in this?

3. How can you recognise your own feelings and how these influence your practice? What help do you need to make the necessary changes?

CHAPTER 9

THE REFLECTION, OBJECTIVE, MOVEMENT AND ACTION (ROMA) MODEL©: A NEW PARADIGM FOR ANTI-RACIST SOCIAL WORK PRACTICE

Dan Allen and Allison Hulmes

The Gypsy, Roma and Traveller Social Work Association

Romani and Traveller people have been saying for many years that they want social workers to promote their human rights and social intercultural inclusion. To do this, social workers must be better equipped with the knowledge, values and skills needed to recognise and challenge racism and to build opportunities for restorative practices.

In 2020, The Gypsy, Roma and Traveller Social Work Association was established to develop world-leading knowledge and support for social workers and allied professionals working to engage Romani and Traveller people. We develop restorative practices that help build and maintain positive healthy relationships, resolve difficulties and repair the harm caused by centuries of racism.

Antigypsyism and aversive racism

Within this chapter, the term 'Romani' includes 'Roma' and 'Romani Gypsies'. The term 'Traveller' specifically refers to 'Irish Travellers'. For readers seeking a more comprehensive introduction, Allen and Adams' (2013) foundation text provides insights into the unique cultures and challenges faced by 'Roma,' 'Romani Gypsies' and 'Irish Travellers' within the British context.

Our association has sought to understand and theorise the relationship between Romani and Traveller communities and social work (Allen et al, 2021; Unwin et al, 2023; Marsh et al, 2024). Much of this research recognises that social workers tend to place Romani and Traveller people as 'outsiders' who challenge the dominant ideologies of child welfare (Allen and Hulmes, 2021). Romani and Traveller families, often associated with the notion of 'The Stranger' (Simmel, 1950) are – Powell (2016) contends – continually 'Othered' and stigmatised by social workers as part of an 'established-outsider figuration' that maintains a 'sizeable power imbalance' between Romani and Traveller people and social work practice.

Research also shows that inequalities in social work can be reproduced through the perpetuation of racist stereotypes about Romani and Traveller cultures. This is recognised in the literature as 'antigypsyism' and described by the European Commission against Racism and Intolerance (2015) as:

> a specific form of racism, an ideology founded on racial superiority, a form of dehumanization and institutional racism nurtured by historical discrimination, which is expressed, among others, by violence, hate speech, exploitation, stigmatization and the most blatant kind of discrimination.

Antigypsyism exists when social workers behave in a way that's openly hostile towards or critical of Romani and Traveller people. When a social worker uses negative stereotypical views to talk about or represent a 'Gypsy' culture, they can also normalise antigypsyism as they dehumanise Romani and Traveller people. One other possible explanation for the sizeable power imbalance between Romani and Traveller people and social work is aversive racism.

The concept of aversive racism has been derived from Kovel (1988), who distinguished implicit racism from the traditional form of explicit racism, which he called 'dominative racism'. According to Kovel (1988, p 54), the dominative racist 'acts out bigoted beliefs [as the] the open flame of racial hatred'. Aversive racists, in comparison, might sympathise with victims of injustice, support the principle of equality and regard themselves as non-prejudiced, but, at the same time, possess negative feelings, views and beliefs about others. Gaertner and Dovidio (2005, p 618) explain:

> The fundamental premise of aversive racism is that many Whites who consciously, explicitly, and sincerely support egalitarian principles and believe themselves to be non-prejudiced also harbor negative feelings and beliefs about Black and other historically disadvantaged groups. These unconscious negative feelings and beliefs develop as a consequence of normal, almost unavoidable and frequently functional, cognitive, motivational, and social-cultural processes.

In contrast to antigypsyism, aversive racism is a subtle form of prejudice that can alter the attitudes of social workers. As shown by Allen and Hulmes (2021), aversive racism can be identified when a social worker genuinely believes they uphold the principles of anti-oppressive practice but feels fearful and helpless when interacting with members of the Romani and Traveller community. An example of aversive racism and antigypsyism is presented in the following case story taken from Allen and Riding's (2018) research:

CASE STORY

Róisín's application for Special Guardianship

My name is Róisín. I am an Irish Traveller and I am 56 years old. I am looking after my grandson under a Special Guardianship Order because his mother can no longer care for him. Getting the Special

$\longrightarrow$

Guardianship Order was a terrible experience for me. I have buried three of my children, experienced domestic abuse and now live in brick-and-mortar housing, away from my family and community, because that is what the social worker said I had to do if I wanted to be considered a suitable carer for my grandson. Despite these challenges, when I applied for Special Guardianship the local authority initially refused.

There were lots of reasons why the local authority refused my application at first, but the most upsetting reason was because I am an Irish Traveller. During our meetings, the social worker told me that my grandson was not meeting his cognitive abilities because he was living in an Irish Traveller culture. She also said that my grandson suffered harm because of my aggressive behaviour and the lack of emotion I give to him. In another report, an expert witness psychologist wrote: 'I was oppositional and unable to be emotional because I was an Irish Traveller and because I lack cognitive development as seen in Travellers'. In the report, the psychologist wrote that the 'Irish Traveller culture influenced my Grandson's development adversely'. To my knowledge, there is no research to prove the claim that Irish Travellers lack cognitive development. But, based on these words, the local authority refused my application for Special Guardianship because they believed that my grandson needed to be saved from the 'Irish Traveller culture'.

Eventually, and after a week-long court hearing, my barrister managed to challenge all the negative reports about me. I was awarded the Special Guardianship Order, but nothing has ever been done about the racist things that were said about me. This was all just brushed under the carpet. I suppose that the social worker and psychologist who tried to remove my grandson are still out there writing racist things about Travellers.

The examples of antigypsyism and aversive racism presented in the case story represent the legacy of a social work system constructed by non-Romani and Traveller people for non-Romani and Traveller people. Although the case story presents a range of concerning practices, we don't think social work needs reform. But we do think practices need to be reframed. Within this context, restorative supervision, rather than a well-rehearsed recommendation for cultural competence, emerges as the potential solution to overcome antigypsyism and aversive racism.

Restorative supervision

In social work, restorative supervision is the process used to support good practice and take account of professional values, codes of conduct and continuing professional development. Unlike traditional models of supervision, which tend to focus on monitoring and evaluation, restorative supervision emphasises the importance of building relationships, fostering learning environments and addressing the well-being of social workers and the communities they serve. A crucial component in the provision of restorative practice emerges as supervisors enable social workers to identify oppression within the existing socio-political order of public protection and child welfare services. Although restorative supervision can be conducted in more than one format, we believe it should consist of four stages. Facilitated by a skilled supervisor, each stage should focus on the need to address conflict, repair harm and promote opportunities to heal the social divisions caused by centuries of racial inequity (see Figure 9.1).

Stage 1: Reflection

Applied to the earlier case story, 'Stage 1: Reflection' offers critical reflection to identify and analyse social inequities and the power structures that maintain them. Reflection encourages discussion about antigypsyism and more critical thought about the impact of assumptions, values and actions. To support anti-racist practice in the first stages of the conversation, attention is given to the reason for social work involvement with Róisín and her family and the presence of interlocking structural inequalities. This would include the intersectional impact of antigypsyism, ecological and social injustice, poverty, sexism and gender-based violence.

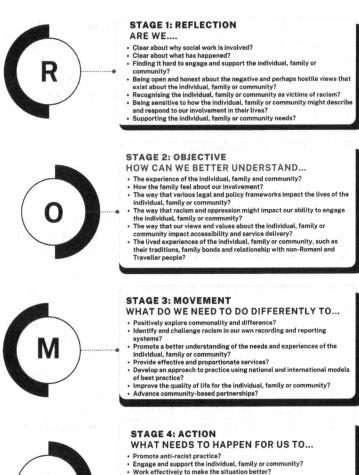

STAGE 1: REFLECTION
ARE WE....
- Clear about why social work is involved?
- Clear about what has happened?
- Finding it hard to engage and support the individual, family or community?
- Being open and honest about the negative and perhaps hostile views that exist about the individual, family or community?
- Recognising the individual, family or community as victims of racism?
- Being sensitive to how the individual, family or community might describe and respond to our involvement in their lives?
- Supporting the individual, family or community needs?

STAGE 2: OBJECTIVE
HOW CAN WE BETTER UNDERSTAND...
- The experience of the individual, family and community?
- How the family feel about our involvement?
- The way that various legal and policy frameworks impact the lives of the individual, family or community?
- The way that racism and oppression might impact our ability to engage the individual, family or community?
- The way that our views and values about the individual, family or community impact accessibility and service delivery?
- The lived experiences of the individual, family or community, such as their traditions, family bonds and relationship with non-Romani and Traveller people?

STAGE 3: MOVEMENT
WHAT DO WE NEED TO DO DIFFERENTLY TO...
- Positively explore commonality and difference?
- Identify and challenge racism in our own recording and reporting systems?
- Promote a better understanding of the needs and experiences of the individual, family or community?
- Provide effective and proportionate services?
- Develop an approach to practice using national and international models of best practice?
- Improve the quality of life for the individual, family or community?
- Advance community-based partnerships?

STAGE 4: ACTION
WHAT NEEDS TO HAPPEN FOR US TO...
- Promote anti-racist practice?
- Engage and support the individual, family or community?
- Work effectively to make the situation better?
- Promote the safety and well-being of the individual, family or community?
- Ensure that negative and perhaps hostile views do not influence the assessment?
- Protect the individual, family or community from racism?
- Understand how the individual, family or community describes and experiences our involvement in their lives?
- Challenge structural inequalities?

Figure 9.1 The Reflection, Objective, Movement and Action (ROMA) Model©: a framework for restorative supervision

Adapted from Allen et al (In Press)

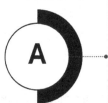

Stage 2: Objective

Stage 1 emphasises the importance of understanding the hidden presuppositions that can shape the relationship between Róisín and social work. But Stage 2, the identification of 'Objective', supports conversations about social work involvement and how to tackle antigypsyism. During Stage 2, the supervisor facilitates opportunities for the social worker to articulate and gain some control over inequalities and uncertainty. This paves the way for positive engagement, clear explanation and clarity of both expectation and momentum for change.

If social workers realise that actions used to exclude and marginalise Róisín can create a fearful response towards intervention, Stage 2 offers a closer analysis of the differences created and maintained by hierarchies of oppression. Objectives can then be set to effect social change and justice through individual and/or collective activism. The inclusion of the 'Objective' stage is, therefore, an important precursor to 'Movement', allowing individuals to locate and scaffold their ability to effect change, both at an individual and collective level.

Stage 3: Movement

Stage 3 advances a framework for accepting antigypsyism and the views, options and experiences of Róisín while building momentum for movement and transformational change in line with legislation and core professional values.

To promote conversations that are cooperative and productive, Stage 3 encourages the social worker to think about ways to develop community, manage conflict and repair relationships that have been damaged by centuries of racism. Throughout Stage 3, the conversation focuses on the importance of confronting racism through the recognition that Róisín and her grandson must have access to the resources they need to live healthy, happy and fulfilling lives.

Stage 4: Action

The 'Action' stage requires a great deal of courage as social workers try to engage the struggle for racial justice while concurrently understanding racism, discrimination and antigypsyism. Although social workers might struggle to repair relationships that have been damaged by prolonged oppression and racism on their own, it's hoped that by moving through Stages 1, 2 and 3, the 'Action' agreed at Stage 4 will enable social workers to stand together in solidarity with Róisín in the evolution of a pro-Romani and Traveller rights-based approach to social protection and child welfare.

To facilitate opportunities for all involved to be positively motivated, Stage 4 offers sufficient time to discuss the reasons for social work interventions and decide on a fair and proportionate solution. At all times, the conversation centres on the principles of participation, collaboration and restorative justice. Once the actions have been identified and agreed upon, the conversation can move on to review and evaluate the 'action plan' with respect to safety, legal concerns and associated resources, moving back to Stage 1, as and when required.

Conclusion

The conversations facilitated using the ROMA Model are unlikely to eliminate antigypsyism on their own. Most Romani and Traveller people experience extreme socio-economic deprivation and inequality and need additional support to develop positive relationships with social work and social workers. As such, the model may be best used to complement rather than replace current structures and systems of supervision, casework management and review. Used alongside formal methods of supervision, models of case discussion, team meetings and direct work with Romani and Traveller individuals, families and communities, we believe that the ROMA Model© can be used to address conflicts, repair harm and promote opportunities to heal the social divisions caused by centuries of racial inequity.

Reflective questions to move us forward

1. What is antigypsyism and how does it impact social work with Romani and Traveller people?
2. What examples of antigypsyism and aversive racism can you identify in Róisín's case story?
3. How can you use the ROMA Model® to practise in a way that is rights-based, anti-racist and congruent with international social work ethics and values?

References

Allen, D and Adams, P (2013) *Social Work with Gypsy, Roma and Traveller Children*. London: CoramBAAF.

Allen, D and Hulmes, A (2021) Aversive Racism and Child Protection Practice with Gypsy, Roma and Traveller Children and Families. *Seen and Heard*, 31(2): 44–67.

Allen, D and Riding, S (2018) *The Fragility of Professional Competence: A Preliminary Account of Child Protection Practice with Romani and Traveller Children*. Budapest: European Roma Rights Centre.

Allen, D, Bolton, J, Dove, J, Hulmes, A, Kidd, C, Moloney-Neachtain, M, Rees, I, Rogers, M, Smith, A and Unwin, P (In Press) A Scoping Review of Social Work with Romani and Traveller Communities: Introducing the ROMA Model®. *European Journal of Social Work*.

Allen, D, Dove, D, Hulmes, A and Moloney-Neachtain, M (2021) The Romani and Traveller perspective. In Moore, T and Simango, G (eds) *The Anti-Racist Social Worker: Stories of Activism in Social Care and Allied Health Professionals* (pp 61–75). St Albans: Critical Publishing.

European Commission against Racism and Intolerance (2015) *ECRI General Policy Recommendation No. 15: On Combating Hate Speech*. Strasbourg: European Council.

Gaertner, S L and Dovidio, J F (2005) Understanding and Addressing Contemporary Racism: From Aversive Racism to the Common Ingroup Identity Model. *The Journal of Social Issues*, 61(3): 615–39.

Kovel, J (1988) *White Racism: A Psychohistory.* London: Free Association Books.

Marsh, H, Hulmes, A and Peacock, J (2024) Inclusive Curriculum Design, Anti-Oppressive Pedagogy and Gypsy, Traveller, Roma, Showmen and Boater Communities. In Morgan, J and Rogers, C (eds) *Supporting Gypsy, Traveller, Roma, Showmen and Boaters (GTRSB) in Higher Education: A Handbook for University Staff in the United Kingdom on Developing Good Practice* (pp 54–68). London: Work and Employment Research Unit, University of Greenwich.

Powell, R (2016) Gypsy-Travellers/Roma and Social Integration: Childhood, Habitus and the We-I Balance. *Historical Social Research*, 41(3): 134–56.

Simmel, G (1950) *The Sociology of Georg Simmel* (Translated and Edited by Kurt H. Wolff). Glencoe, IL: The Free Press.

Unwin, P, O'Driscoll, J, Rice, C, Bolton, J, Hodgkins, S, Hulmes, A and Jones, A (2023) *Inequalities in Mental Health Care for Gypsy, Roma, and Traveller Communities, Identifying Best Practice*. NHS Race and Health Observatory.

CHAPTER 10

SEEING AND BEING: THE INVISIBLE MINORITIES

Victoria Hart

A 'hidden' minority

Part of being Jewish is living with the burden of the impact of racialised hate. A 'racism' that excludes Jewish experiences will always be one that builds on stereotypes and tropes which negatively impact Jewish people.

Being a 'hidden' minority brings advantages. I can choose whether to reveal my Jewishness. People don't 'know' when they look at me. But that brings challenges as well. I have been exposed to open antisemitism from those who would probably have guarded their tongue if they'd known about my Jewishness, thinking I would happily nod along with their assessment of the perfidy of Jewish people.

Jewish people don't 'fit' into a neatly constructed Western model of 'race' based on necessarily visible difference. We can be and are of many different skin colours and physical characteristics. But we are more than a 'religion' of choice. One is born into or consciously joins the Jewish 'people'; because we are a 'people', a 'nation', a 'tribe' – language that doesn't quite fit into Western definitions of how and who we should be.

Some Jewish people present as White, others as Black. Intersectionality as it relates to Black Jewish people will place an additional responsibility and burden of silence, discrimination and racism.

If you met me, you wouldn't know I'm Jewish unless I chose to share that information with you. My name isn't stereotypically Jewish. This vital, unchanging part of my identity is something that you may never know about, unless I choose to tell you.

Fredrickson (2015) emphasises the racism and the development of racial antisemitism affecting Jewish people from the late nineteenth century in Central Europe, saying:

> Pigmentation ... is not the only supposedly indelible mark of difference upon which racism can be based, as the history of antisemitism clearly demonstrates.

The perception of Jewish people as a 'race' was enough to trigger racialised hatred, including a genocidal hatred which targeted Jewish people. Understanding racism must include a consideration of the experience of the Jewish people. We are a perceived 'race' which has experienced, and still experiences, intergenerational trauma. As Rees (2017) writes in his seminal history of the Holocaust:

> Never before in history, I think, had a leader decided that within a conceivable time frame an ethnic religious group would be physically destroyed, and that equipment would be devised and created to achieve that. That was unprecedented.

Being Jewish in the UK

A record number of antisemitic incidents were reported in 2023 (Community Security Trust, 2024) across the UK, with a rise of 147 per cent from 2022. The Jewish community in the UK is tiny. We count for 287,000 (less than 0.5 per cent) out of the England and Wales population of 59.6 million (Office for National Statistics, 2021). The census figures may under-represent the number of Jewish people in this country. This is partly due to how the question is phrased as it doesn't record both faith and ethnicity, and the Jewish community extends to those who might identify as practising the religion. But also, Jewish people in Europe have an aversion to being counted by government bodies. Call it intergenerational trauma if you like.

In practice, this means many social workers may not have had the opportunity to meet and work with Jewish people, either as colleagues, friends, or people who access social work services. This increases the risk of assumptions, stereotypes and deeply set prejudices to embed in a culture if it goes unchallenged.

Learning about and challenging assumptions about Jewish people in the UK is a stepping stone to understanding minority groups and communities that may not be recognised in more formal teaching settings.

CASE STORY

I'm going back to when I was working in an older adults' mental health team as well as practising as an Approved Mental Health Professional (AMHP). Our local authority ran a small specialist AMHP rota for older adults, so during my 'day role' I would often have to prioritise Mental Health Act Assessments.

Many of the older people I worked with didn't have families living nearby. Maybe this was indicative of the cost of housing in central London rising beyond the possibilities of most working people.

I worked with a couple, Mr and Mrs Jones. I say 'a couple', although only Mr Jones was 'allocated' to me as he'd developed depression after retiring, and it had reached the point where he'd been admitted to hospital a number of times. But I supported his wife too, as she was his main carer. Their children, loving and attentive, weren't local but visited regularly and I'd developed a good relationship with them both.

During the third year we'd been working together, Mr Jones was watching the snooker from his chair, and I went to the kitchen to help Mrs Jones with the tea. This was her chance to talk about things on her own.

$\rightarrow$

I'd told her I was taking leave for a few weeks, including our next scheduled visit, because it was the Jewish New Year. I wasn't in the habit of telling people I was Jewish, not because it wasn't something important to me, but because it was irrelevant to my role as a social worker.

I'd known her for about three years at this point, having been with the family through some of their darkest periods, including signing the papers and arranging admission for her husband under the Mental Health Act. As care coordinator I'd supported them through illness of family members and the isolation that mental illness and caring can bring.

'*Are you Jewish?*' she said.

This was a question I always struggled with. Whether or not to be open is a decision to be made every time this is asked because you know you're taking a risk each time you answer.

'*Yes*', I said, because to be honest, I'd already explained the reason for my absence, so I wasn't giving her any new information.

'*Don't tell my husband*,' she whispered.

I nodded, not wanting to break her train of thought.

'*He doesn't like Jews.*'

I nodded again. Her tone was apologetic, so I didn't pursue it. This was a man with whom I'd built up a strong relationship over the years and it seemed like a matter that wasn't relevant to our relationship going forward.

'*My father was Jewish*,' she whispered to me. She nodded towards the living room where her husband sat. '*I never told him.*'

'*My father came over here when he was young and he married my mother in St John's. I don't think he ever intended us to know, he never told us even when he was on his death bed, it was his "shameful secret" I think – but when he died we found some old books, some letters and … they were his documents, his identity documents from when he came over. He never told us but it changed something within me when I found out. It changed who I am – but I always think of him carrying it with him all his life. There were reasons he didn't want us to know.'*

Mr Jones called for his tea and we went back into the room, with teas, biscuits and a bond that was never explicitly mentioned again. I worked with them for another 18 months or so before I left.

Hiding identity through fear, for years, decades even, can internalise the racism which exists in society. As Jewish people, we don't just have decades of this but can reach back further in time through the generations. Intergenerational trauma is real, and understanding it is a key to being better at 'doing' anti-racist social work.

Moving past the obvious

The experience of hiding identities is one that can be extrapolated beyond day-to-day practice. It was purely by chance that I happened to share an aspect of my own identity that led Mrs Jones to share with me part of who she was. But it's an experience I've reflected on many times and it's helped me think through other scenarios about hidden identities and how that links to anti-racist practice.

We don't know who might be hiding or why. And we can't second-guess, especially if we're working in faster-paced environments that don't allow much scope for building relationships over years. But we can be aware there may be hidden aspects to the people with whom we work, their cultures, their communities and their beliefs.

Jewish people live with intergenerational trauma which has led to families and immigrants trying to protect their children from the discrimination they've faced, thinking they might be able to 'hide in plain sight'. This was partly the experience of my parents who both changed their surname to a more anglicised version and chose some of the most 'English'-sounding forenames they could.

'You can always hide it,' they said, but I chose not to. Other minoritised people whose differences are more obvious don't have the privilege of being able to make that decision. Being part of a history where each generation has been targeted and subjected to increasingly sophisticated methods of discrimination and extermination leads to fear.

Doing anti-racist social work includes being aware of the possibilities of unspoken racialised traumas which come to light as misdirected hate and confusion grow. Being Jewish has affected me profoundly. I always think about those who are hiding the secrets of generations that they are still afraid to disclose.

As Horn (2021) stated in the aptly named *People Love Dead Jews*:

> Some other people might go to Holocaust museums to feel sad, and then to feel proud of themselves for feeling sad. They will have learned something officially important, discovered a fancy metaphor for the limits of Western civilization. The problem is that for us, dead Jews aren't a metaphor, but rather actual people that we do not want our children to become.

We still exist within living memory of the industrialised genocide of a racialised group of people, the Jewish people; two-thirds of those who lived in Europe were killed. This came after decades, centuries, millennia of persecution. Increasingly, in times when we see people pulling 'Nazi' comparisons out of their hate as a casual indication of the disapproval of a particular political line, we won't be able to learn the lessons until we listen to the voices of the Jewish people and the families of the Jewish people who live on, understanding the impact of the traumas that have been exacerbated by disbelief or suspicion.

We never know, as social workers, who we might be working with and what they may not feel safe sharing with us.

Learning from invisibility

So what can we learn from my story and what changes can we implement? It may not have changed my interactions with the Jones family at all, but it helped me understand how to work with invisible minoritised groups. I am more sensitive to the group that I have grown up around, but this is a feeling, thought, reflection that can be extrapolated to many different situations.

What do we do to reassure the people we work with that we're safe for them to share their identity with us? How do we show that we can be respectful custodians of the inner secrets of their lives and use that information to better serve, rather than further distance?

Would I, in these times of increasing antisemitism, be happy for my social worker to know I was Jewish, were I to need one? Possibly not, based on the social media feeds I see of some of the social workers and social work organisations I know.

We can all challenge our prejudices and assumptions. We can be allies for the people whose background, ethnicity and beliefs we might know. But we can also make it clear that it's safe for them to be around us. We can ease some of that longstanding trauma and fear of othering and we can work to build people up.

Drawing on this teaches us we need to both understand differing experiences of racism by different ethnically marginalised groups, and to remember the specific experiences of Jewish people of colour who experience intersectional oppression and racism.

Fredrickson (2015) states:

> Antisemitic racism ... persists and, despite the Holocaust and the creation of the State of Israel, retains the capacity to do harm. Hate groups in many countries continue to believe the Hitlerian myth that the world is threatened by a Jewish conspiracy. The World Wide Web is filled with their ranting.

A society where people feel free to be who they are without hate, and fear of hate, is the society we should aspire to as social workers.

Reflective questions to move us forward

Many differences of race and ethnicity may be invisible. What impact does that hidden, and possibly shameful, aspect of one's identity have on the ability to understand what an individual or family needs from social work input?

1. How can we ensure an awareness of invisible intergenerational trauma which might be unspoken when we work with people? How might this impact parenting or caring relationships?

2. While victims of racism and racialised discrimination may sometimes be evident, what can we do in our conversation and relationship building to ensure that we don't make assumptions on the basis of one aspect of someone's identity?

Further reading

Bassi, C (2023) *Outcast – How Jews Were Banished from the Anti-Racist Imagination*. London: No Pasaran Media.

Langman, P F (1999) *Jewish Issues in Multiculturalism*. Oxford: Aronson.

Nelson, M K (2022) Shame, Silence, and Family Secrets: How Enduring Antisemitism Created False Identities. [online] Literary Hub. Available at: https://lithub.com/shame-silence-and-family-secrets-how-enduring-antisemitism-created-false-identities/ (accessed 9 January 2025).

Rich, D (2023) *Everyday Hate*. Hull: Biteback Publishing.

References

Community Security Trust Antisemitic Incidents Report 2023 – Blog. [online] cst.org.uk. Available at: https://cst.org.uk/news/blog/2024/02/15/antisemitic-incidents-report-2023 (accessed 9 January 2025).

Fredrickson, G M (2015) *Racism: A Short History*. Princeton, NJ: Princeton University Press.

Horn, D (2021) *People Love Dead Jews: Reports from a Haunted Present*. New York City: W W Norton & Company.

Office for National Statistics (2021) Religion, England and Wales – Office for National Statistics. [online] www.ons.gov.uk. Available at: www.ons.gov.uk/peoplepopulationandcommunity/culturalidentity/religion/bulletins/religionenglandandwales/census2021 (accessed 9 January 2025).

Rees, L (2017) *The Holocaust – A New History*. London: Viking.

CHAPTER 11

CO-CREATING A MODEL FOR ANTI-RACIST SUPERVISION

Shabnam Ahmed and Jo Williams

This chapter captures the authors' shared interest and passion for anti-racist supervision. Our stance is that *if you can do good anti-racist supervision, you can do good supervision; it's as simple and as complex as that* (Williams et al, 2022). We introduce ourselves and our partnership, discuss three significant issues of racism in social work and present a model for exploring anti-racist supervision, illustrated through a case story.

Introductions to us and our positions

Shabnam – I identify as a South Asian, Pakistani British Muslim woman. I am a passionate social worker, practice educator and an independent trainer. Dove and Fisher's (2019) call to change the parts of the world we can touch through the ideas of relational activism inspired me to think about two areas in which I deliver training – anti-racism and supervision. I decided to focus on the supervisory space as a manager. I believed this was one of the spaces where I could wield influence through embedding the principles of anti-racism to benefit the supervisee, their practice and therefore outcomes for the adults, children and families we came into the profession to walk alongside.

Jo – I am a White British woman and grew up in the south of England, where I have worked in social work and social care settings for 30 years. My social work practice focus has been working with children and families, although my passion has specifically been supervision. I am particularly interested in the psycho-social and emotional landscape of supervision and how supervisors can create a safe haven and secure base for supervisees (Williams, 2023). I am an aunty to three Brown children, and they have taught me much about racism in British society. Recently, I have been thinking more deeply about what it means to be an anti-racist ally and how we can become anti-racist in our practice as social workers and particularly in supervisor and leadership roles.

How we came together

In 2022 we came together with a shared interest in anti-racist supervision, which led to a writing partnership. Both of us deliver supervision training and there are some messages we share regularly about good practice, which we thought would be helpful to merge in this chapter. We hope we've shared some practical actions that supervisors of all races, no matter what the supervisory dyad looks like, can do to ensure supervision is a space which embeds the principles of anti-racism throughout. We've drawn on our experiences and knowledge of racism and anti-racist allyship to set out our ideas for a model of anti-racist supervision. We recognise that understanding what makes anti-racist organisations in social work is still developing and our ideas about anti-racist supervision practice will grow as this unfolds.

Anti-racism – issues for supervision

Structural inequality

A range of statistics build an unequal picture for Global Majority (Black, Asian and minoritised ethnic) children and adults' experiences of growing up and living in the UK today. Black children are 3.5 times more likely to be excluded from school and 4 times more likely to be arrested than their White peers; and Black people see more than twice the unemployment levels than White people, with 46 per cent of households in the UK being in poverty compared to 20 per cent of White households (Barnardo's, 2020). Systemic racism and structural inequality also mean there's an under and over representation of different groups of vulnerable people from the Global Majority receiving services across services (eg Bansal et al, 2022). These factors put the issue of racism at the core of case supervision.

Social workers' experiences of racism at work

Racism is taking its toll on Global Majority social workers in England. More than a quarter of social workers in England faced racism from clients and one in ten from colleagues or managers. Racism led to increased anxiety for 20 per cent, worsened mental health for 13 per cent and prompted 10 per cent to consider quitting (What Works for Children's Social Care, 2022). This makes racism a significant issue for both the well-being and retention of social workers, where supervision is a key mechanism for support.

Barriers to career progression

Supervisors need to be mindful of the workplace experiences of Global Majority staff, particularly in relation to barriers to career progression. Global Majority social work students take longer to pass their placements and their Assessed and Supported Year in Employment. Global Majority social workers are less likely to progress to senior leadership roles (Bernard, 2020), and workplace racism is seen as a reason for this. These facts put the issue of institutional racism at the core of staff supervision and Bernard (2020) challenges managers to contemplate strategies to address this historical predicament.

Developing a model for anti-racist supervision

Social work supervision has been defined as *'a process by which one worker is given responsibility by the organisation to work with another worker(s) in order to meet certain organisational, professional and personal objectives'* (Morrison, 2005, p 32). The relationship and working alliance is the main vehicle for doing this effectively. Therefore, anti-racist supervision requires a supervisor who can hold power and knowledge of oppressive forces in mind, with a willingness to be courageous and actively initiate conversations to highlight these and find ways to mitigate systemic and institutional racism.

Such a task is rooted in both relational and emotional literacy skills. Institutional racism can become a barrier to maximising this capacity so it helps to apply a framework for an anti-racist approach to ensure that there's not a relational shortfall which leaves oppression and inequality unaddressed. We've drawn on Morrison's (2005) Integrated '4x4x4' Model and Tedam's (2013) Mandela Model to consider practical ideas for developing a model of anti-racist supervision. This is an idea that Shabnam has been exploring through her work and developed further through conversations with Jo.

Morrison's (2005) '4x4x4' supervision model is often cited across supervision policies in the UK (see Figure 11.1). The original model comprises three elements, each with four considerations. At its core resides the four stakeholders ultimately benefiting from supervision. Integrated within the model lies Kolb's four-stage reflective learning cycle, highlighting the reflective facet of supervision. The outermost layer sets out the functions of supervision.

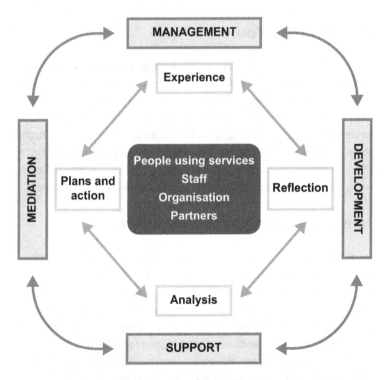

Figure 11.1 Integrated Supervision Model (Adaptation from Morrison, 2005) – infographic, with acknowledgements to the Department for Education-funded Practice Supervisor Development Programme

The Mandela Model (Tedam, 2013) (see Figure 11.2) uncovers synergies between the practice placement experiences of Black African students, linked to their relationship with their practice educator. The model incorporates anti-discriminatory and anti-oppressive practice and has been helpful in illuminating the functions of supervision from Morrison's 4x4x4 model by placing an anti-racist lens on it.

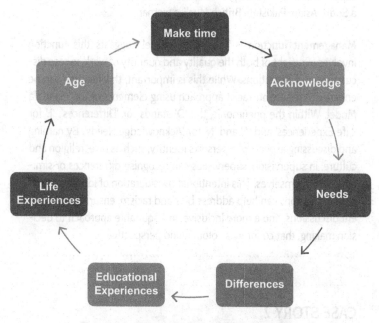

Figure 11.2 The Mandela Model (Tedam, 2013)

The next part of the chapter focuses specifically on the functions of supervision, using a case story example to illustrate a practical application.

Functions of anti-racist supervision – utilising Mandela

CASE STORY 1

Although we are co-authors and peers, we invite you to imagine us as a supervision dyad, with Jo as the supervisor and Shabnam as the supervisee. As a reminder, Jo is a White British woman and Shabnam is a South Asian, Pakistani British Muslim woman.

Management function – The 4x4x4 model suggests this function involves oversight of both the quality and quantity of work, ie case discussions and allocations. While this is important, this function can be enriched with an anti-racist approach using elements of the Mandela Model. Within the pneumonic, the 'D' stands for 'Differences', 'L' for 'Life Experiences' and 'A' and 'N' for 'Acknowledge Needs'. By naming and discussing aspects of a person's identity, such as race, religion and culture, in supervision, supervisees can recognise differences or similarities to themselves. This intentional consideration of identity within case discussions can help address bias and racism, ensuring transparent discussions, and a more inclusive and equitable approach to decision making, that counters a colour-blind perspective.

CASE STORY 2

During a case discussion, Jo invites Shabnam to share cultural or religious factors that might influence her approach to the situation. Shabnam explains the importance of 'izzat' (family honour) in South Asian culture and particularly to this family. She shares her personal experience with this concept. Jo acknowledges Shabnam's insights and takes a curious approach, as this is not something she has come across before. This ensures transparent and inclusive decision making, recognising and valuing the unique cultural context of the supervisee and the family that is being discussed. This approach not only enriches the management function of supervision, but also fosters a more equitable and supportive environment for both the supervisee and the people we are working with.

Development function – This function is intended to consider both horizontal and vertical growth for social workers. An anti-racist approach would consider the research on barriers to progression for Global Majority social workers when discussing their development. Providing space for social workers to identify their needs ('A' and 'N' for Acknowledge Needs). Early conversations about racial differences ('D' for Differences) foster openness and curiosity. Reflecting on my experience as a South Asian woman (Shabnam), I believe that a lack of intentional discussions with supervisors hindered my progression to a management role for 20 years. Anti-racist supervisors should be courageous, critical, creative and curious (O'Neill and del Mar Fariña, 2018). Using the Mandela Model, particularly 'A' for Age, which can refer to both chronological and how long someone has remained in a position, and 'A' and 'N' for Acknowledge Needs, can enhance this approach. Greater supervisor curiosity and acknowledgement of my specific needs and barriers might have accelerated my career progression.

CASE STORY 3

During a monthly supervision session, Jo enquires if there are any cultural or systemic barriers affecting Shabnam's career progression. Shabnam highlights challenges, including internalised oppression for Global Majority social workers, and shares her personal struggles with limited mentorship opportunities and recognition early in her career. Jo acknowledges Shabnam's feelings about this and asks what specific actions they can take to support Shabnam's career progression and to overcome these barriers. Recognising her privileged position as a White woman in management, Jo acknowledges that while she has faced barriers, they are Different from

$\longrightarrow$

those encountered by Shabnam. This ensures a developmental process which is transparent and inclusive, recognising and valuing the unique cultural context and professional barriers faced by Shabnam. This approach enlivens the development function of supervision by embedding the principles of equity.

Support function – This function of supervision is crucial for all social workers due to the emotional labour involved. For Global Majority social workers, this burden is compounded by societal racism, depleting their emotional resources. Anti-racist supervisors, using the Mandela Model's 'L' for Life Experiences and 'A' and 'N' for Acknowledge Needs, must show professional respect, love, care, kindness and compassion. They should 'M' for Make Time for containment and for supervisees to feel enabled to share any experiences of racism. They should also be ready to take appropriate action.

CASE STORY 4

During a supervision agreement/contracting conversation or at any point in the relationship, Jo could ask Shabnam 'how would I know when to worry about you?', 'what would I notice?', 'how would I know if you were concerned about racism?', 'what has helped you to discuss your needs in supervision previously?'. It may not be possible in the moment for Shabnam to answer these questions, but it would let her know that Jo is interested. Throughout the supervision relationship, Jo will need to continue to be curious about Shabnam's well-being and how racism specifically may be impacting on her.

Mediation function – This function positions the supervisor as a bridge between the supervisee and the organisation. Using the 'dance floor to the balcony' analogy from adaptive leadership, imagine the supervision space representing the dance floor. Here, the anti-racist supervisor, through the 'M' for the Make Time element of the Mandela Model, sets aside time to understand and address challenges arising from racism. They then take these insights to the balcony, where they meet with senior managers and have an opportunity to influence strategic and actionable change within the organisation. In terms of anti-racism, supervisors also help the organisation understand its people and their needs to become genuinely anti-racist. They can use their agency to advocate for the staff, and the adults, children and families that social work sits alongside, fostering a robust anti-racism policy and culture.

CASE STORY 5

It is likely that through having built a trusting and empathic supervision relationship, Shabnam will have highlighted to Jo how she has been impacted by racism in her role and within the organisation. This is an opportunity for Jo to think about how to better meet Shabnam's needs through supervision conversations. It will also give Jo information about racism within the organisation and she can consider how to shape and influence the practice system at other levels, such as within the team, and the service area and at an organisational policy level. This means she can draw on insights from Shabnam directly to act as an ally and use her position of power and privilege to influence change.

Key messages

Becoming anti-racist requires continuous perseverance in self-reflection, persistent self-awareness, consistent self-criticism and regular self-examination (Kendi, 2019). This applies to everyone, no matter what their race, but White supervisors in particular must be willing to take the lead and do this work, walking alongside their colleagues from the Global Majority.

To be intentional about anti-racism and supervision requires consideration of the role of learning, reflective and practice spaces in which we can be uncomfortable, and brave. The process of becoming an anti-racist supervisor requires courage, vulnerability and a willingness to be imperfect and clumsy.

Reflective questions to move us forward

1. Having read the chapter, what comes to mind from your racial perspective as a supervisor, what are you confident about and how might you position yourself differently?

2. Which supervisees come to mind and why? Which supervisees do you think about the least? What do you need to consider in light of this?

3. Which adult/child/family comes to mind and how might you focus your next supervision/conversation on race?

Further reading

Ahmed, S and Black & Ethnic Minority Professionals Symposium (2022) *Anti-Racist Supervision Template.* Available at: https://basw.co.uk/about-social-work/psw-magazine/articles/anti-racism-supervision-template-eradicate-colour-blind (accessed 25 February 2025).

Boahen, G (2023) Understanding Racial Dynamics in Supervision. In Moore, T (ed) *Principles of Practice by Principal Social Workers.* St Albans: Critical Publishing Ltd.

Practice Supervisor Development Programme [open access] Equity, diversity and inclusion Archives – Practice Supervisor Development Programme Repository. Available at: https://practice-supervisors.rip.org.uk/asset-category/equity-diversity-and-inclusion/ (accessed 25 February 2025).

References

Bansal, N, Karlsen, S, Sashidharan, S P, Cohen, R, Chew-Graham, C A and Malpass, A (2022) Understanding Ethnic Inequalities in Mental Healthcare in the UK: A Meta-Ethnography. *PLoS Medicine*, 19(12): e1004139.

Barnardo's (2020) How Systemic Racism Affects Young People in the UK. Available at: www.barnardos.org.uk/blog/how-systemic-racism-affects-young-people-uk (accessed 9 January 2025).

Bernard, C (2020) Addressing Barriers to the Progression of Black and Minority Ethnic Social Workers to Senior Leadership Roles. Available at: https://practice-supervisors.rip.org.uk/wp-content/uploads/2021/01/StS_KB_Addressing_Barriers_Progression_of_Black_and_Minority_Ethnic_SWs_FINAL.pdf (accessed 9 January 2025).

Dove, B and Fisher, T (2019) Why Relational Activism Might Bring Hope and Light to Social Change – Greta, Jacinda and Us. Royal Society for the Arts. [online] Available at: www.thersa.org/discover/publications-and-articles/rsa-blogs/2019/03/why-relational-activism-might-bring-hope-and-light-to-social-change (accessed 9 January 2025).

Kendi, I X (2019) How to be an Antiracist. London: One World.

Morrison, T (2005) Staff Supervision in Social Care. Brighton: Pavilion.

O'Neill, P and del Mar Fariña, M (2018) Constructing Critical Conversations in Social Work Supervision: Creating Change. Clinical Social Work Journal, 46(4): 298–309.

Tedam, P (2013) The MANDELA Model of Practice Learning: An Old Present in New Wrapping? Journal of Practice Teaching and Learning, 11(2): 60–76.

What Works for Children's Social Care (2022) Anti-Racism Survey Report. Available at: https://whatworks-csc.org.uk/research-report/anti-racism-survey-report/ (accessed 9 January 2025).

Williams, J (2023) Supervision as a Secure Base: The Role of Attachment Theory within the Emotional and Psycho-Social Landscape of Social Work Supervision. Journal of Social Work Practice, 37(3): 309–23.

Williams, J, Jennings, S and Ahmed, S (2022) Anti-Racist Supervision (film). [online] Available at: https://practice-supervisors.rip.org.uk/assets/anti-racist-supervision/ (accessed 9 January 2025).

CHAPTER 12

REIMAGINING PRACTICE EDUCATION: EXAMINING RACE, POWER AND PRIVILEGE

Antonia Ogundayisi

Education was about the practice of freedom.

(hooks, 1994, p 3)

As a Black woman, social worker and practice educator, hooks' philosophy resonates deeply for me. I believe in education as a tool to sharpen and inspire liberatory movement for both educator and student.

Imagine social work fostering both personal and collective freedom. Imagine supervision giving permission for radical, conscious and critical thought, anchored in hope that change *is* possible for the racially oppressed. That together, you and I, as educators, can strangulate the beast of racism.

Imagine. Now, believe.

Believe it's possible.

Now, act.

Act as an instigator of change.

Imagine – Believe – Act.

As a service manager in a large local authority, I oversee an anti-racist strategy for social care. The intersection of race with practice education is not hypothetical, but real and critical. Every word in this chapter is my activism. I want each reader, whether a student, educator, leader or visitor, to leave with hope.

Practice education: the racial context

The significance of practice education within social work cannot be overstated. As practice educators, we serve as the gatekeepers to our profession, playing a pivotal role in preparing future social workers to deliver high-quality care and support to people, families and communities.

Yet research indicates that placement experiences of Black and ethnically diverse students often differ markedly from those of their White peers. Black students report that practice learning environments, especially where White peers and leadership are predominant, tend to reinforce racist attitudes and behaviours (Fairtlough et al, 2014). Newly qualified social workers from Black and ethnically diverse backgrounds are more likely to face difficulties in completing their Assessed and Supported Year in Employment (ASYE) compared to their White counterparts (Skills for Care, 2024). Research shows they often contend with both 'invisibility' and 'hypervisibility' in the workplace. This paradoxical position means their contributions and presence are not acknowledged, yet at the same time they face surveillance by their managers, leading to greater scrutiny in the workplace (Obasi, 2021). Black students also experience a lack of support and belief from their practice educators about their potential and experience ongoing exhaustion from battling racial fatigue (Bartoli et al, 2008; Dillon and Pritchard, 2021).

Such findings are concerning. They underscore the pressing need for anti-racist practice to be a central component of social work practice education. Without deliberate efforts to address these disparities, our profession risks perpetuating the very inequities we seek to dismantle.

Race, racism and social work education

Critical Race Theory (CRT) offers a paradigm to understand the relationship between race and society. CRT proposes that race remains a dominant factor within educational practices (Ladson-Billings and Tate, 1995). This conveys that the relationship between social work and racism is composite. Social work is often caught between advocating for oppressed communities while also reinforcing oppressive structures. In 2020, the murder of George Floyd re-ignited discourse about racism within social work, yet as a profession we still do not have enough knowledge about systemic racism. Organisational structures in which we operate are ill-equipped to respond to racist incidents and Black students and social workers experience a lack of support from managers (Cane and Tedam, 2022). With this awareness, practice educators must become racially conscious to understand, resist and dismantle racism on an individual, interpersonal and systemic level.

To support this, I've developed questions to help practice educators think about how their racial identity might inform their assessment of students' abilities. These questions can be used in personal or group supervision or within appraisal processes.

Reflective questions

1. Self-reflection on racial identity

- *What does my own racial identity mean in the context of my role as a practice educator?*

- *How might my racial identity shape my interactions with students who are of a different racial background to my own?*

- *How does race shape dialogues when there are commonalities between me and my students?*

$\longrightarrow$

---

2. Understanding Whiteness and privilege

- *How might I centre Whiteness in my approach to teaching, supervision or assessment?*

- *What assumptions may I make about the student's behaviour, competency or attitude that may be influenced by a White experience or perspective?*

3. Assessing practice learning

- *Does my language and behaviour invite and welcome theory and knowledge that's outside a Eurocentric lens?*

- *Are diverse voices, perspectives and experiences included in the curriculum?*

- *Do I encourage students to openly challenge dominant narratives and give voice to the oppressed?*

It's not enough to simply acknowledge or verbalise differences. To truly be an anti-racist practice educator, we must actively dismantle practice, policies, procedures and behaviours that uphold White supremacy.

Supporting students

Black and ethnically diverse students completing placements in predominately White organisations may face additional challenges during placement. For instance, overseas students may experience accent bias, cultural differences, institutional racism and anxiety (Fairtlough et al, 2013). By being attentive and vigilant, we may notice that Black students may not share their thoughts and opinions for fear of being disregarded or discredited. They may begin working from home more to seek emotional safety. They may not ask for help for fear of being seen as not good enough. Anxiety may manifest differently for each person. Being emotionally attuned as educators means we understand these might not be performance issues, but well-being issues. Documenting the psychological and emotional experiences of students may help us effectively respond to the unique challenges of Black and ethnically diverse students.

The practice educator/student dynamic operates within a wider organisational context; their relationship is operating within wider organisational cultures, patterns, habits and behaviours. If the wider organisation is not talking about race and racism, practice educators may not speak up. Normalising conversations about race and racism and collating precise race-based data should be a part of our organisational culture as it creates an anchor for us as educators to initiate discussions about race from the outset of the placement.

Opening the relationship with attention to race and racism has a profound impact on students who may have never been acknowledged in this way before. The following questions can be a helpful way to introduce the subject of race and racism at the start of the practice educator/student relationship.

Reflective questions

1. How does it feel for you to be in the minority within a predominately White institution?

2. What does it feel like for you to be managed by a White manager, have a White tutor and White colleagues?

3. Is there anything a White manager has done in the past that worked well, and if so what was it?

Remember, such questions are not formulaic but can be asked amid an evolving warm, trusting and supportive relationship. From my experience of being a student, I experienced the warmth and genuine investment from my practice educators. This was demonstrated by their body language, frequent check-ins about my well-being and the intentional allocation of a Black female practice educator. Representation matters. My success was their success. It's a feeling. How do our students *feel* about us?

Tedam (2011) has conducted extensive research to understand the experience of Black and diverse students within practice learning settings. She developed the Mandela Model to help practice educators explore similarities and differences between themselves and students. The model proposes the following as a framework for anti-oppressive practice:

- M – Make Time

- AN – Acknowledge Needs

- D – Differences

- E – Educational Experiences

- L – Life Experiences

- A – Age

CASE STORY 1

Kudzai, a mature Black female social work student, joins your team to complete her 100-day placement. Kudzai migrated to the UK from Zimbabwe five years ago. Your team and organisation are predominately comprised of White employees. Kudzai has strong values centred around community and family-based support.

Consider:

- How will Kudzai feel a sense of belonging in your team?

- How will the induction process support Kudzai's understanding of policies and procedures, in alignment with her learning style?

- How do the racial dynamics within the team impact Kudzai's ability to speak up and share ideas?

- How are cultural differences explored openly within supervision?

- How are Kudzai's cultural perspectives within casework seen as valid?

CASE STORY 2

Timothy is a White British male social work student. He'll be working with a family of Pakistani ethnic origin.

Consider:

- How might the family see Timothy and what may his race and gender represent to them?

- How can you help Timothy to prepare to work with the family in an anti-racist way?

- Are there any potential biases or assumptions that Timothy may bring to his work?

- Which areas in the organisation does Timothy have to openly discuss race?

- Does Timothy show good reflection in his portfolio or reflective logs about this?

Race and racism are not just a discussion for Black and ethnically diverse students. Racial dialogues must also be normalised for White students. The student's portfolio provides a fantastic opportunity for students to evidence how they have considered power, privilege and anti-racism with their peers and service users. What does it mean to be a White social worker?

Black practice educators

The experiences of Black practice educators are not homogenous and cannot always be generalised. However, Black practice educators may struggle trying to survive within White supremacist cultures yet also trying to show up authentically in their leadership. It's therefore important to acknowledge that for some Black practice educators, 'everyday racism' can impede them from rightfully asserting their power and authority in their role as educators. For Black educators working within predominately White institutions, there may be personal risk when race is discussed. If we, as the people that make up institutions, become racially conscious, greater curiosity can be given to whether the expertise, thoughts and contributions of Black educators are heard, respected and valued.

CASE STORY 3

Monroe is a Black male practice educator. He has been a practice educator for six years. One of his students asks him questions about child protection and though Monroe responds, he notices the student constantly checks with a White manager about the information he is given.

Consider:

- How might racial biases be influencing the student's decision to seek confirmation from a White manager?

- In what ways can Monroe's expertise and authority as a Black practice educator be recognised and valued in the practice learning environment?

- How does the racial diversity of the organisation affect Monroe's interactions and the respect he receives from the student?

- Are there institutional practices in place to address and challenge racial attitudes, which may include the student's action of seeking confirmation from a White manager?

- How does the organisation foster a culture that supports and values the perspectives of Black practice educators like Monroe?

Embedding anti-racist practice

Good practice requires an unswerving focus on anti-racist practice (Bhatti-Sinclair, 2011). As practice educators, we are key players in creating an ongoing learning culture. Alongside consistent self-reflexivity, we can influence practice, procedures and policies to incorporate an anti-racist lens.

This can include, but is not limited to:

- keeping anti-racist practice as a rolling agenda item for directors and seniors or within high-level meetings;

- conducting frequent audits of the educational curriculum or practice academy to ensure that anti-racist pedagogy and learning materials are included;

- embedding and facilitating ongoing reflective discussions about race and racism;

- ensuring clear organisational policies, procedures and pathways that state how the organisation and learning institutions respond to racist incidents, including racism from service users.

Acting it out

The Practice Educators Professional Standards (PEPS) state that practice educators must ensure there is no stigmatisation or disadvantage within assessment processes and that educators must demonstrate applied knowledge and understanding of the significance of racism (BASW, 2022). The current outcomes for Black and diverse students show these values are not effectively enacted. Because of the powerful relational dynamics between us and them, students may remain quiet about any lack of competency in our approach to anti-racism. And so, the racist practice of the practice educator may persist.

While we relentlessly advocate for systemic change, *we* can change. If we are to truly contribute to empowering oppressed communities and gatekeeping our profession, it must begin with us.

We must ask ourselves the difficult questions – *how many of* my *students who are Black have been passed on their placement successfully?* Quantify it. Unveil the story behind each student. As social work educators, we must move beyond simply teaching, to being anti-racist activists who maximise our own and our students' ability to become racially conscious. This intentional standpoint goes far beyond mere knowledge exchange but towards true liberation for Black and ethnically diverse people and communities who are fatigued from being dehumanised. In this regard, practice education does not just stop in hefty portfolios but reaches living rooms, classrooms and communities. An anti-racist practice educator means the oppression of Black and ethnically diverse people is responded to and thus, practice education instigates the practice of freedom.

Here are some tips on how we can begin.

- Name how race and racism will be discussed as part of the learning agreement contract.
- Utilise key milestone meetings, such as placement reviews, to provide leverage to revisit conversations about race.
- Explore whether students are experiencing incidents of racism.
- Become familiar with the policies and protocols that can be referenced when incidences of racism occur.
- Be aware that as practice educators or university tutors, we can be the perpetrators of racist behaviour.
- Ensure full clarity for the student about governance routes with named specific people who can be contacted.
- Remember that when instances of racism have occurred, racial trauma should be considered and how this can impact the student's well-being and placement performance.
- Ensure there are safe spaces for Black students where representation is visible, and buddies, mentors and coaches can be accessed.
- Draw on the resources and knowledge from other parts of the service.
- Normalise conversations about race and racism within team meetings.
- Ensure there are Racist Abuse/Incidents Logs that track racist incidents.
- Conduct self-appraisal – where are you on your anti-racist journey and have you grown? If so, how would students know?
- Advocate for an organisational-wide Anti-Racist Policy.

Your commitment

Use this acronym to help you to think about where you can start today.

[E] – Educate yourself about Whiteness, White supremacy and systemic racism.

[D] – Dismantle White supremacy.

[U] – Understand the unique experiences of Black students.

[C] – Call out racist behaviours, practices and policies.

[A] – Activate your influence.

[T] – Transform the educational curriculum.

[O] – Observe your thoughts, biases and assumption.

[R] – Remember it is a marathon, not a sprint.

Reflective questions to move us forward

1. Would you be described as an anti-racist practice educator? Explain why/why not.

2. How can you actively support Black and ethnically diverse students in overcoming the systemic barriers they face within social work education?

3. What steps can you take today to strengthen your commitment to anti-racism?

References

Bartoli, A, Kennedy, S and Tedam, P (2008) Practice Learning: Who is Failing to Adjust? Black African Student Experience of Practice Learning in a Social Work Setting. *Journal of Practice Teaching & Learning*, 8(2): 75–90.

BASW (2022) Practice Educator Professional Standards (PEPS). [online] Available at: https://basw.co.uk/policy-practice/standards/practice-educator-professional-standards-peps (accessed 9 January 2025).

Bhatti-Sinclair, K (2011) *Anti-Racist Practice in Social Work*. London: Bloomsbury Publishing, pp 139–40.

Cane, T C and Tedam, P (2022) 'We Didn't Learn Enough about Racism and Anti-Racist Practice': Newly Qualified Social Workers' Challenge in Wrestling Racism. *Social Work Education*, 42(8): 1–23.

Dillon, J and Pritchard, D J (2021) Relational Learning and Teaching with BME Students in Social Work Education. *Social Policy and Society*, 21(1): 93–105.

Fairtlough, A, Bernard, C, Fletcher, J and Ahmet, A (2013) Black Social Work Students' Experiences of Practice Learning: Understanding Differential Progression Rates. *Journal of Social Work*, 14(6): 605–24.

hooks, b (1994) *Teaching to Transgress: Education as the Practice of Freedom*. New York: Routledge.

Ladson-Billings, G and Tate, W F (1995) Toward a Critical Race Theory of Education. *Teachers College Record: The Voice of Scholarship in Education*, 97(1): 47–68.

Obasi, C (2021) Black Social workers: Identity, Racism, Invisibility/ Hypervisibility at Work. *Journal of Social Work*, 22(2): 479–97.

Skills for Care (2024) Assessed and Supported Year in Employment (ASYE) Child and Family.

Tedam, P (2011) The MANDELA Model of Practice Learning: An Old Present in New Wrapping? *Journal of Practice Teaching & Learning*, 11(2): 60–76.

CHAPTER 13

TOWARDS ANTI-RACIST CHAIRING OF SOCIAL WORK MEETINGS IN THE UK

Dr Arlene Weekes

It is more important than ever that social work decision-making processes are free of racism. This requires that chairs and attendees of social work meetings operate with full awareness of the many racial disparities which, despite some advances in recent years, remain embedded in UK social work practice. But this awareness is not easy to achieve: the many subtle forms of racism, such as implicit biases and microaggressions, often permeate the dynamics of meetings. This chapter demonstrates how a clear anti-racist position can engender an inclusive meeting environment that empowers and values diverse perspectives and marginalised voices.

Why promote anti-racist chairing practices?

My own experience of attending and chairing meetings has led to an interest in the development of anti-racist chairing practices. Over a period of more than two decades of experience as chair of adoption and fostering panels, it had become clear to me that many professionals in social care operate under the illusion of complete impartiality, even though personal experiences and cultural backgrounds invariably shape all our perspectives, and this observation led to reflection on how personal biases and assumptions influence panel members' judgements – especially when they believe themselves to be 'non-judgmental' (Weekes, 2021). These reflections, in turn, led to further investigation, through doctoral research (Weekes, 2021), of the underlying dynamics at play in social work meetings, and subsequent work on how personal beliefs, values and prejudices could impact fairness in decision making. The result was a profound personal desire for others to embrace anti-racist chairing principles, and enable a space where all voices are respected and cultural differences are acknowledged and valued.

The theoretical background to anti-racist chairing

Although this chapter is concerned with real-world issues – specifically, illustrations of how racism manifests itself in social work meetings, and how it can be combatted – some theoretical background is relevant and useful. It should be noted, for example, that, while there is a substantial body of literature on the subject, the most pertinent theories to the approach taken by this chapter are the constructivist frameworks, which propose that race is a social construct, with no scientific basis, which is used as a means of classifying people based on power and privilege (Ifekwunigwe et al, 2017). Historically, this construct has been used overtly, as a rationale for exploitation and discrimination. Now, however, it is used (for much the same reasons) more covertly. This chapter understands racism as a systemic power, not merely personal prejudice, although it recognises that everyone can be prejudiced regardless of colour. Nonetheless, the most pernicious and damaging form of racism is that which is based on skin colour. 'Whiteness' describes the way White culture, beliefs and identity are treated as the standard against which all others are measured (hooks, 1997). Thus, to be anti-racist, there must be an emphasis on confronting racist policies, challenging White dominance which reinforces systemic bias, and working towards racial equity (Kendi, 2019).

The concept of constructivism has significant relevance to the specific issue of chairing meetings in today's social work environment. Several studies, for example, have demonstrated the need, when chairing, to understand that attendees construct meaning, and process information, about individuals through the lens of stereotype-based expectations. Other major causes of decision-making bias include subjectivity, pre-existing beliefs, emotional responses and personal biography. To chair in an effective anti-racist manner, it's necessary to actively challenge these biases.

Another important concept, in the context of social work meetings, is that of groupthink (Janis, 1982), which can lead to flawed decision making by a closed-minded, cohesive group due to internal pressures for unanimity and suppression of dissent. Although there are practical mechanisms that can be deployed to minimise the effects of groupthink, there is little doubt that it remains a powerful obstacle to unbiased, open discussions and fair decision making.

How racism manifests itself

To contextualise the next section, it is worthwhile to review one of the most controversial government-commissioned reports of the century. This was the Commission on Race and Ethnic Disparities (CRED), more commonly termed the Sewell report, as it was chaired by the Black chairman Lord Tony Sewell. It is probably unnecessary to remind readers of the circumstances surrounding the death of George Floyd in May 2020; more relevant, from the perspective of this chapter, are the conclusions of the report. These conclusions not only downplayed the impact of structural, political and social disadvantage that exist in UK society, but also concluded that the claim that the UK is institutionally racist is 'not borne out by the evidence'. For many Black people and communities who know firsthand the impact of systemic racism in their daily lives – for example, disparities in education, employment, healthcare and policing – the report directly refutes their lived experiences.

This is also true for me as my stories relay, as with other Black social workers and those in allied professions, who, whenever they raise issues of racism, experience a dismissal of their concerns. They are often told that they have 'misinterpreted', or are overreacting, and usually face retaliation in the form of adverse performance reviews and lack of career opportunity. Any concern which is shown is superficial and political, designed to 'wave away' the issue. Rarely, if ever, does the expression of such concerns result in substantive reform.

CASE STORY 1

From a meeting attendee's viewpoint

Addressing anti-racism in professional meetings

Background: A Black service manager, working in a county council where 95 per cent of the staff were White and there was no other Global Majority service manager, experienced being undermined by team managers and other service managers. The service manager had successfully contributed to turning around the service, earning the respect of many colleagues.

Challenges: Despite having 30 years of experience as a practitioner, including 24 years as a manager, more than 17 years in the fostering and adoption field and also being a published author, the service manager experienced significant challenges from two team managers who were subordinate to her role. They questioned her knowledge and expertise, leading to a notable incident where they sought confirmation from an external source, which subsequently validated the service manager's advice. Nonetheless, there was no acknowledgement or humility when they were found to be wrong.

Subsequently, during a meeting chaired by two of her managers, the service manager was frequently disrespected by being interrupted and silenced. Although her comments were minimal, some team managers accused her of bullying. This accusation was relayed to her by her manager with no prior discussion or investigation into the context, or the behaviour of those who interrupted her. This feedback marked the beginning of a shift in the service manager's relationship with all levels of colleagues and the organisation.

As the only Black senior manager among a local group of Asian service managers, the Black service manager experienced a significant incident of internalised oppression while in an executive meeting attended by a group of predominately White service managers. Internalised oppression is a concept used to characterise actions and viewpoints that are derogatory against oneself or other members of one's own racial group or identity and that have their roots in the group's historical narrative. When the Black service manager later raised this matter during one of the 'support' meetings, the reaction was one of astonishment that one of the group members would act in such a way, thus highlighting a lack of awareness and sensitivity to the dynamics of racial discrimination within the organisation.

Resolution: Despite her commitment to the job and her success in the role, the lack of support and the inability to address racist aggression led to the service manager's resignation. Her manager, upon hearing of this decision, was visibly upset, apologising for the 'bullying' comments and the latter's failure to adequately address the issue.

Lessons learned: This story illustrates the importance of anti-racist practices in professional settings, highlighting the need for organisations to ensure a safe and inclusive environment where all voices are valued, and any form of racial discrimination is addressed promptly and effectively.

The response to accusations of bullying, or other inappropriate behaviour, should involve a thorough investigation and context analysis rather than accepting the accusations at face value, based on 'Whiteness'.

Key takeaway: The case emphasises that anti-racist chairing is not just about preventing overt racism, but also about creating a culture where subtle forms of racism are addressed and all employees, regardless of status, feel supported, valued and respected.

CASE STORY 2

From the meeting chair: addressing anti-racism in a fostering and permanence panel meeting

Background: A virtual meeting of the Fostering & Permanence Panel aimed at determining the suitability of the long-term relationship between two Black children (River, five; Petra, seven) and their current (White) foster carer, Amy.

Challenges: The meeting highlighted the complexities of transracial fostering, raising questions about the children's cultural needs, their contact plan and the health and safety conditions in their foster home. There was also uncertainty about Petra's paternity and the implications for her identity. Additionally, Amy's description of River as an 'angry little boy' raised concerns about the language used and the need for therapeutic support.

There was also a clear lack of thorough family research on the children, suggesting that the agency had not fully explored all placement options. This lack of due diligence could lead to further complications in addressing the children's needs, especially in terms of considering the cultural differences between the White foster carer and two Black children.

Resolution: The Black chair did not agree to the match, as it did not conform to National Minimum Standard 2 of the Fostering Regulations 2011: 'Promoting a positive identity, potential and valuing diversity through individualised care'. The chair expressed her dismay about how these issues are being dealt with. However, the ultimate decision of the panel (by majority) was to approve the match for long-term foster care, noting that the children were settled in Amy's care and that there was clear affection between her and the children. The panel also advised the agency on areas needing further attention, including obtaining more information on paternity and the support of Amy in managing a transracial placement.

Lessons learned: The case story highlights how the chair can use processes to avoid groupthink. By allowing each panel member to express dissenting views, a split decision was reached. The story also under-scores the importance of addressing cultural and identity needs in fos-ter care, especially in transracial placements.

Key takeaway: For social work meetings to be effective in address-ing anti-racism, it is essential to create an environment where group-think is avoided, and each member can prioritise the cultural needs and identity considerations of the children concerned. This requires an open and objective chair, careful consideration of language, thorough family finding and ongoing support if transracial placements need to be made. By addressing these factors, fostering panels can contribute to a more inclusive and anti-racist approach to social work.

Towards anti-racist chairing: a summary

The stories in this chapter provide real-life examples of chairing, and highlight the challenges faced in ensuring that anti-racist practices are always followed. To address these challenges, those chairing panels must adopt an approach that emphasises equality, cultural competence and inclusivity by facilitating meetings in a manner that:

- sets clear expectations of conduct in relation to what is, and is not, acceptable;

- uses collaborative techniques to ensure an inclusive meeting, ie agendas and attendee representation;

- raises awareness by openly speaking about race and anti-racism;

- challenges bias, insensitivity, microaggressions and 'Whiteness';

- welcomes marginalised voices;

- supports and empowers those who experience racism, thereby providing psycho-logical safety;

- equips all attendees with skills to address racism.

In short, an effective anti-racist chair needs to embrace diverse perspectives and address implicit biases by fostering an inclusive meeting environment that facilitates dialogue and empowers marginalised voices. This is achieved by establishing guidelines and effective communication strategies, together with anti-racist policies that promote equality by addressing structural, systemic racism and microaggressions.

Reflective questions to move us forward

As a final thought, here are some questions for you to reflect upon, based on the issues discussed earlier.

1. If you were to chair a meeting, what steps would you prioritise to ensure a more inclusive and anti-racist environment?

2. If you were a chair or attendee at a meeting, what steps would you take to identify and address your own implicit biases?

3. How can personal judgements be improved to ensure effective professional anti-racist practice in meetings?

References

hooks, b [1992] (1997) Representing Whiteness in the Black Imagination. In Frankenberg, R (ed) *Displacing Whiteness* (pp 165–79). Durham, NC: Duke University Press. doi: 10.1215/978082270-006.

Ifekwunigwe, J O, Wagner, J K, Yu, J H, Harrell, T M, Bamshad, M J and Royal, C D (2017) A Qualitative Analysis of How Anthropologists Interpret the Race Construct. *American Anthropologist*, 119(3): 422–34. https://doi.org/10.1111/aman.12890.

Janis, I L (1982) *Groupthink: Psychological Studies of Policy Decisions and Fiascoes*. 2nd edn. Boston: Houghton Mifflin.

Kendi, I (2019) *How to be an Antiracist*. London: Bodley Head.

Weekes, A (2021) The Biographic and Professional Influences on Adoption and Fostering Panel Members' Recommendation-Making. *Adoption & Fostering*, 45(4): 382–97. https://doi.org/10.1177/03085759211058359.

Weekes, A (2021) There's No Such Thing as Non-Judgemental. *Professional Social Work*, May: 28–9.

CHAPTER 14

PRACTICE LEARNING AND REVIEWING SERVICE (QUALITY ASSURANCE)

Noshin Mohamed

My journey through the identity maze: what does 'other' even mean?

I never fit into a neat box when it comes to data collection; I always tick 'other' for my ethnicity. This experience of being 'othered' has stayed with me throughout my life. As a woman of dual heritage, I take immense pride in my diverse background, but this also means I often find myself grappling with a complex relationship to my identity. The more I delve into the subject of identity, the more intricate it becomes. Last year, I read a book by Kwame Anthony Appiah on identity and realised how little I actually know about the complex world of identity and how it shifts and changes over time. I often wonder how my son, who has a more mixed background than me, may perceive his identity and relationship to it as he progresses through life. This personal journey has shaped my understanding of inclusion and representation, highlighting the limitations of conventional data collection methods that fail to capture the rich, multifaceted nature of individual identities.

Quality assurance (QA) in social work

My journey towards integrating anti-racist practices within the quality assurance (QA) service began somewhat unexpectedly. My role is to oversee the quality assurance function within a children's and young people's service in a London borough. Initially, the subject of anti-racism within QA didn't cross my mind until I started to scrutinise audit methodologies and data more closely, a curiosity sparked by attending a 'Data Ethics Club', organised through Bristol University. This group challenged me to think about the ethical implications of audits and the use of data to influence change and so much more.

The power of QA in social work is often underestimated. Typically, QA is associated with compliance, often perceived as the 'big brother' ensuring that procedures, policies and legislation are followed. Some colleagues laughingly have compared QA to the watchful slug from *Monsters, Inc*. However, this perception underlines the immense influence QA holds as it's capable of shaping systems, influence, organisational culture, practices and even policies. By systematically evaluating and monitoring processes, QA can identify areas for improvement, highlight best practices and ensure accountability at all levels. This power extends beyond merely checking processes; it can be harnessed to drive systemic change. When QA integrates anti-racist and inclusive principles, it becomes a powerful tool for promoting equity and justice. By setting high standards for anti-racist practice and holding systems accountable, QA can ensure that social work not only adheres to policies and procedures but also champions fairness and inclusivity. Sounds great, doesn't it? But how do you even begin?

Integrating anti-racist practices in QA

Trying to embed anti-racist practice within the QA service was far from easy. It began with a collaborative effort where my peers and I deconstructed our entire audit process, from scoping and methodologies to recommendations. At every stage, we considered how to incorporate anti-racist principles. We challenged ourselves further, questioning whether race is solely to do with one's skin colour and whether racism can be directed towards individuals from White backgrounds. To say it was overwhelming is an understatement.

What we found was that anti-racist principles can be incorporated at every step of the way in QA. For instance, when scoping a thematic audit, questions can be asked about bias, both of the auditor/reviewer and in the data set (was this randomly selected, or were case files specifically given?). How do you consider the auditor's knowledge of the subject area, and if they have gaps in their knowledge about race and culture, how does this influence an audit outcome? It felt daunting to achieve, but there was hope to enhance our responses to anti-racist practices within QA. Working in one of the most diverse boroughs in London means race is not a factor to be ignored in audit activities; it must be addressed head-on, with the courage to have difficult conversations. In the end, with the guidance of an extremely knowledgeable person who asked us to reflect on why we wanted to embed anti-racist practices into our QA framework in the first place, the answer was simple – these issues are not being addressed effectively, and QA has the power to change that.

So, a simple solution was struck: just one recommendation. At the end of each audit, one recommendation is now made that aligns with anti-racist and inclusive practice. Why? Because change needed to start somewhere. Creating meaningful change doesn't require an overhaul of the entire system. It can start with something as simple as one recommendation. Just one recommendation can prompt senior managers to consider race within the system, sparking the conversation about systemic change.

CASE STORY

In QA, while we often capture information about ethnicities, I have always questioned the purpose if no action follows. We must always remember that we are handling someone's record, someone's personal story. Ethically, we must ask ourselves, 'What is my responsibility in relation to this person's data and story?' How will this information be used to support system change, and what is my role as the auditor or reviewer in ensuring this happens?

While we are still in the early stages of implementing the recommendations, recently, I conducted an audit focusing on children entering care. The audit revealed a disproportionately high number of children from Black, Black British, African and Caribbean heritages.

$\rightarrow$

To understand this in context, I compared our findings with local demographic data from the Office for National Statistics (ONS). This comparison confirmed that the percentage of children from these heritages entering care was significantly higher than their representation in the local population. However, identifying actionable recommendations to address this disparity at a local level proved challenging. I pondered for what felt like forever on what we could do to address this issue. Here are two areas that I considered (you may be able to think of more!).

- Conducting a further audit activity to understand the primary reasons for children from Black, Black British, African and Caribbean heritages entering care.

- Conducting a collaborative audit with our families to identify potential barriers to accessing early intervention and support.

This audit has taught me that we don't need to generate sparkly, immediate recommendations to achieve change. This process is not a sprint; it's a marathon. There will be times when we need to push and dig deeper to truly understand the situation before implementing meaningful actions. We know that individuals from Global Majority backgrounds are likely to face numerous inequalities, whether due to immigration status, class or education. Therefore, when we start to address race within QA activities, we also begin to address these systemic and structural inequalities.

The need for a collaborative approach in QA

We often like to simplify a complex world into neat boxes, yet I don't fit neatly into the ethnicity box! This tells you that although quantitative data is important, it does not offer the richness of qualitative data, which includes stories, experiences and narratives. Increasingly, a number of local authorities have started using co-design and co-production principles. There is great power in this as services are then designed by the people and communities they are meant to serve.

Applying this principle to audit activities means listening to voices and ensuring that the human experience behind the data is truly captured. By ensuring that feedback and experience are captured from communities we want to hear from, we can enrich our understanding and shape our services and interventions accordingly. It is simple to say, but ensuring inclusivity for those who may not otherwise participate or give feedback is crucial. For instance, this includes providing interpreters for those who have English as a second language to participate meaningfully. It becomes about being intentional with how much you value the narrative and how to support participation.

Reflections on anti-racist methodologies in QA

There is so much that can be done, and it feels as though the data science and research community has delved far more into anti-racist practices than we have in QA within local authorities. In a recent trip to New York, I picked up a book entitled *Decolonizing Methodologies* by Linda Tuhiwai Smith. Upon reading just the introduction, I had to pause, reflect and really think about my positionality when it comes to audit-based activities. I was born and raised in London, and my education is from the Western world, so I see the world through my own unique lens. But when it comes to audits, how coloured are we by our unique experiences? When we think of the audit scope, are we simply following processes, or are we challenging the system to think differently so that we can really advocate for voices that are otherwise not always brought to the forefront? We must consider various cultural practices and understand that what we may deem normal, others may not, and vice versa.

The QA journey is just starting!

As previously mentioned, I am still in the early stages of a larger journey towards implementing anti-racist and inclusive practices into QA. However, I am actively trying to incorporate what I have learned so far. I am currently designing an audit activity based on the methodologies from this book. The audit will focus on understanding why children from the Global Majority are being diagnosed with SEN or mental health needs only when it reaches a crisis point. Having worked in different boroughs, I have observed significant differences in parents' understanding of their child's rights, their ability to advocate and their familiarity with the system. These disparities are particularly pronounced among parents from the Global Majority background.

The audit will employ a collaborative approach, aiming to eventually co-design earlier access to support, but I am keen this be done *with* rather than *to* those that will be using the support. To achieve this, I want to hear the stories of parents, carers and children about their journey to diagnosis. By understanding their experiences, my aim is to identify where changes are needed within different systems to facilitate earlier intervention and support. We often talk about the Social Graces framework (Burnham, 1993) and intersectionality factors, but applying the principles behind this systemic practice can be very powerful. It involves not just naming the GRACE but truly reflecting on what is happening for both the individual and the collective.

Often, managers and social workers may see an audit as an additional task that needs to be done. What gets lost is the power of this tool to make a difference in practice and to the individual whose case file is being audited. Auditors have a responsibility to support reflection, to really think about social graces and intersectionality factors. Sometimes, merely this reflection can change the direction the case is heading in. Auditors have the power to not only support reflective practices and challenge existing processes, but also to provide feedback on systemic themes, thereby fostering broader organisational and systemic changes. For practitioners whose work is subject to audit, it's important to recognise that the focus isn't solely on the individual. Instead, it's about understanding how we, as a collective system, come together to drive and support meaningful change.

There is still a long way to go the QA system is not perfect – in my view, far from it – but it is about harnessing the power of QA to make a positive difference.

Reflective questions to move us forward

I leave you with these three thoughts.

1. How are you better understanding and integrating the diverse experiences and perspectives of those we serve?

2. In your QA work, do you actively discuss anti-racist practice?

3. And lastly, if you are from QA, how have you built anti-racist practices into your audit activities?

References

Appiah, K A (2018) *The Lies That Bind: Rethinking Identity.*
London: Profile Books.

Burnham, J (1993) Systemic Supervision: The Evolution of Reflexivity in the
Context of the Supervisory Relationship. *Human Systems*, 4: 349–81.

Smith, L T (2012) *Decolonizing Methodologies: Research and Indigenous
Peoples.* 2nd edn. London: Zed Books.

CHAPTER 15

YES, BUT HOW DO YOU KNOW IF ANYTHING IS ACTUALLY CHANGING?

Nimal Jude

Introduction

So, you've got to this stage in the book and might be thinking a variety of things like '*I do this already*' or '*that's a great idea, I'm going to try that*'.

But, how will you know if anything you are doing is actually making a difference?

The journey of anti-racism in social work is crucial for developing and strengthening relationships, not only with those we serve but also within ourselves, our colleagues and the profession as a whole. Anti-racist practice involves understanding the intricate web of relationships that influence and shape our work. This chapter emphasises the importance of evaluating these efforts through asking the right questions, tracking, monitoring, reviewing and improving activity. Robust quality assurance and analysis of the data it produces may already be an established part of service development. This chapter points to the need for specific evaluation on anti-racist initiatives and uses two examples, one at organisational level and one at practice level, to illustrate its importance.

Many of us understand that anti-racism is central to social work because it aligns with the core values of social justice, equality and human dignity. Structural racism refers to systemic inequalities ingrained in societal institutions that favour certain racial groups over others. In social work, this can manifest through biased assessments, unequal resource distribution and discriminatory policies, and little effort and research to appropriately evaluate progress and improve.

Social workers are uniquely positioned to identify and challenge racial injustices, advocating for fair and equitable treatment for all. If we truly want to combat structural racism, we must critically examine practices within our own agencies. Effective evaluation of anti-racist efforts requires clear understanding of these systemic issues and the development of strategies to address them.

In volume one I co-authored a chapter on the implementation of the Social Care Workforce Race Equality Standards (SC-WRES) in 18 Local Authority Children and Adults services (Harvey et al, 2021). What struck me was there were lots of ideas and initiatives on local authority action plans; I'm talking about things like reverse mentoring, support groups for racialised people, anonymised recruitment, training, learning and development. But there was little detail about why specific interventions had been chosen, what differences were anticipated or how they would know whether they had made any difference at all.

Setting goals and intended outcomes

To ensure anti-racist initiatives are effective, we need clear goals and intended outcomes. This involves identification of the specific changes we want to achieve and the impact we aim to have for our workforce and the people we serve.

The following case story is an example of how this might work:

CASE STORY 1

Organisational level

Task: improve work environment for marginalised workforce

You've gathered data from workforce surveys, sickness levels, staff focus groups, appraisals and team meeting discussions. This pooled local evidence shows you that reports of incidents that demonstrate racial bullying and harassment are much higher than you thought. It's only when you've looked at all this data together that you've realised this is a problem which seems to have been going on for some time. You need to address it so you set a goal and work out how it can be achieved.

> **Intended outcome/goal:** Reduce incidents of bullying and racial harassment, increase feelings of safety and inclusion among racialised people in the workplace.

> **Activities:** Implement anti-bullying training for staff and students, create cultural awareness activities, offer space for staff forums, hold listening surgeries, establish better policies to protect people from racial harassment.

You do some research and find there's good evidence that anti-bullying and harassment programmes reduce incidences of bullying and harassment and improve well-being. You decide to commission some training. You'll ensure this training will provide a platform for the workforce to engage in conversations through various channels (one-to-ones, team meetings, listening surgeries). You'll use the information gathered from the conversations and focus groups held after the training and work collaboratively to create some further actions and update your policy and practice which will be reviewed with the staff forum in six months.

$\longrightarrow$

How will you know if this training and the reviewed policy has made an impact?

You can prepare a pre and post training assessment to measure changes in attitudes and behaviours. You should be thoughtful in the questions you ask and they should link directly to the problem you are trying to solve.

You can survey the workforce again and track and monitor notifications of racial harassment. If over six months people report fewer incidents and report that the work environment has improved, you could conclude that the training and organisational learning activity before and after the training has made some difference.

You can compare data across directorates (eg Housing or Finance, etc) and track outcomes in teams in who've completed the training at the start of the training roll-out and those who completed at the end, and you can look for similarities and difference in trends.

However, there may be many other factors that influence your efforts positively or negatively, such as:

A change in leadership. There may be some leaders who aren't perceived as being proactive in tackling racist issues, or the workforce may be feeling disillusioned with the support or lack of it from the People team. These behaviours and perceptions can delay progress. Then suddenly a new leader arrives with fresh energy and ideas or the existing leadership team make a pact, are motivated, committed and decide to behave differently, and this creates a real sense of hope.

National and global issues. I can't overemphasise the impact that racist narratives and activities, in the media, in organised far right demonstrations, by politicians, police, teachers, in the law and legislation (the list goes on) has on our workforce. How you do or don't acknowledge these big events with your teams in public and/or via one-to-one conversations sets the tone of how you are perceived. Don't underestimate the power of acknowledging at the start of a team meeting that there are terrible racist stories in the news at the moment and to say that we know this is hard to watch and hear and have created some opportunities for people to offload and be heard. You might be thinking that if we did this every time the meetings would just be taken up with talking about those things – sad, isn't it? If your workforce are feeling traumatised and drained, how are the people you're supporting feeling? And how are you supporting your workforce to work through some of this so they can be present for the people you serve?

Inconsistency and injustice. This can quickly collapse all your efforts in building an actively anti-racist learning organisation. Someone else in another department goes rogue and acts against policy and there are no consequences to their actions. People make mistakes, sometimes with the best intentions – and sometimes not. How your organisation responds will make or break everything you try to do next.

If any or all of these things are happening in the background when delivering anti-racist training this will also impact on effectiveness. We know training alone doesn't work; behaviour is influenced by many factors, not least how leaders behave individually and collectively. Developing continuous feedback loops where staff can share their experience and suggest improvements, having clear accountability structures to oversee and drive anti-racist initiatives and ensuring voices are heard and issues are acted upon carries a lot of weight. Sounds easy, eh? I'm under no illusions about the challenges of this work and we social workers must continue to lead the way in our local areas and organisations.

Actions

Bring together a cross-level steering group to work on the development or improvement of your anti-racist journey. Make sure there's a high-level senior sponsor chairing or receiving reports on the progress and challenges to help you unlock obstacles. This is two-way accountability.

Understand your local context. Consider your demographics and local issues relating to racism.

Set goals. Think about the short, medium and longer-term goals you are striving to achieve.

Activities and interventions. What will you put in place to help you move towards your goals? Who will help you? Who will hold you to account?

Track progress. When you start these activities what changes would you hope to see? By when? What data can you collect and measure? How will you report progress internally and externally?

These actions will be helpful for readers involved in leadership and workforce development roles. But what of those of you who aren't? How can evaluation help you?

Individual reflection on practice and the use of supervision to reflect on our own behaviours, biases and interactions can help us consider our areas of personal growth. Engaging in discussion and gaining insight from peers and managers not only enhances our own individual accountability but can also ensure anti-racist principles are integrated into daily practice.

The following reflective questions may be helpful:

Reflective questions

Examples of reflective prompts we might use to evaluate our own approach to anti-racist practice:

1. Who is benefiting from this intervention, and how are their lives improving?

2. Reflect on the direct and indirect beneficiaries of your work. Are there individuals or groups who particularly are or are not benefiting from the interventions? In what ways? How do you know? Do you ask them? eg Do you pool all the information from Black families doing a parenting course and look at the results compared

---

with people who identify as White? Who is dropping out of the group? Why? What can you do about it?

3. Why is this intervention important, and what broader impact does it aim to achieve?

4. Consider the significance of your work within the larger context of social justice. What are the broader societal impacts you hope to achieve through your interventions? So, you may make a referral to Family Group Conferencing as the family are experiencing a particular issue relating to significant harm of a child. However, you may also feel it is important that the family are provided the opportunity to increase their social capital and develop strategies to problem-solve in the future.

5. What specific outcomes do we want this intervention to achieve, and how will we measure success?

6. Clearly define the intended outcomes of your initiatives and establish measures for evaluating success. How will you know if your efforts are making a meaningful difference?

7. How will we know if our interventions are working, and what feedback mechanisms are in place to ensure continuous improvement?

8. Implement feedback mechanisms to gather insights from people accessing services and stakeholders. How will you use this feedback to refine and enhance your practice?

CASE STORY 2

Practitioner level

Context and background

A family, consisting of a mother, Amina, and her two children, Malik (14) and Zara (11) had recently arrived from Zimbabwe. They were referred due to concerns about the children's school performance and behavioural issues.

$\rightarrow$

Initial assessment

During initial meetings, it became clear that the family's challenges were exacerbated by their experiences of racism and discrimination. Malik and Zara were facing bullying and racial slurs at school, contributing to their anxiety and behavioural problems. Amina struggled to find employment that matched her qualifications due to discriminatory hiring practices and language barriers.

Intervention and support

Recognising the central role of racism in their difficulties, our intervention was multifaceted:

Education setting: We collaborated with the school to address the bullying incidents, promoting a safer and more inclusive environment for Malik and Zara. This involved anti-bullying training for staff and students, cultural awareness training and implementing policies to protect students from racial harassment.

Employment assistance: For Amina, we connected her with careers services that supported people from African countries. Additionally, we provided resources for further education and certification to enhance her employment prospects.

Mental health support: To address the psychological impact of their experiences, we facilitated access to culturally competent counselling services for the family. This included therapists trained to understand the unique stressors faced by immigrants and racial minorities.

Community engagement: We encouraged the family to engage with local community organisations that offered support networks for African people. These organisations provided social activities, mentorship programmes and legal assistance, helping the family build a sense of belonging and resilience.

Outcomes and evaluation

To ensure our interventions were effective, we implemented a comprehensive evaluation plan. This included:

Tracking progress: We monitored Malik's and Zara's school performance and attendance records. We also tracked Amina's job search progress and participation in job placement programmes.

Feedback mechanisms: We regularly sought feedback from the family through conversations to understand their experiences and satisfaction with the services provided. This helped us identify areas for improvement and adjust our interventions accordingly.

Quantitative measures: We used quantitative measures such as school performance data and mental health assessment scores to gauge the impact of our interventions.

Qualitative measures: We also employed qualitative measures, including case notes, family interviews and focus groups with community organisations, to capture the nuanced experiences and outcomes of the family.

Through these evaluation methods, we observed significant improvements. Malik's and Zara's school performance and attendance improved, and Amina secured a job that utilised her skills, providing stability for the family. The counselling services helped them process their experiences and build coping strategies, while their involvement in the community bolstered their support network.

Conclusion

Evaluating anti-racist initiatives isn't just a task for leaders and strategic planners; it's a call to action for everyone in the organisation. We can't merely allocate resources and expect change; we need to harness the best evidence to drive the transformation we seek. Implementation must be intentional, with the right conditions to let these initiatives flourish. From practitioners to executive leaders, we all hold a critical role in assessing and enhancing our efforts. Through us all actively participating in evaluation, we bring diverse perspectives and insights that make our anti-racist initiatives both relevant and powerful. This united approach builds a culture of accountability and continuous improvement, propelling systemic change.

To those who worry that all this diverts precious time away from working with people and families, know this: this is the essential work we must embrace alongside them. Let us rise to this challenge and forge a legacy of lasting change: if not now, then when? If not you, then who?

Reflective questions to move us forward

1. What can you do to influence your organisation to put specific measures in place to evaluate the impact of anti-racist practice?

2. How will you understand the impact of racism on the individuals and families you work with?

3. Who is holding you to account? Who are you holding to account?

References

Harvey, M, Jude, N and Shafiq, Z (2021) Journey to a Workforce Race Equality Standard. In Moore, T and Simango, G (eds) *The Anti-Racist Social Worker: Stories of Activism by Social Care and Allied Health Professionals* (pp 127–35). St Albans: Critical Publishing.

Index

Printed in the United States
by Baker & Taylor Publisher Services

Printed in the United States
by Baker & Taylor Publisher Services